THAT'S HOW I REMEMBER IT

Jim Roth

To my friend Frank,
7 August 2009
Remember the days!
Best wishes
Jim Roth

DEDICATION

That's How I Remember It is dedicated to Bente Johannessen Roth, my wife of 36 years, and truly the best partner I could ever have found. She is caring, wise and with a great sense of humor. Her support and loyalty make my life complete and fill it with a multitude of happiness. We once had an argument, but it wasn't serious, or worth remembering (wink). Bente is a critic; her wisdom and excellent judgment contribute to the quality of my writings. Thank you, my dear. Let's hope this one is a winner!

I also dedicate, *That's How I Remember It,* to my family members who have helped create these memories. They include Daughter Kim Roth and Granddaughter Katie; Daughter Robin Roth Rose, and Grandsons Jay and Tim; Son James II and Rosela Roth and Grandson James Roth III; Son David and Daughter-in-law Lisa Roth and Grandson Max; and April Cumley (Roth).

I don't see enough of my family as they are widely scattered, living in Virginia, Florida, Alabama, Kentucky and Nevada, but they are always on my mind and in my heart. Memoir writing connects us often and I'm hopeful that members of our family will take up writing family memories for the next generations.

TABLE OF CONTENTS

I. E-S-T-E-L-L-I-N-E
   1. Saturday Nights 1
   2. Farmer Jack...5
   3. Stranger in Town...11
   4. Uniform of the Day..15
   5. The Roth House 17
   6. Snowfall...23
   7. Need a Haircut 29
   8. Learning a Lesson...31
   9. Jim, Rex and Harley 35
   10. Rat Troubles..39
   11. Sliding Trombone 43
   12. Dad's Parlor 45
   13. Coal Heat 49
   14. Estelline Speedway...53
   15. Bloody Adventurers..57

II. FLY WITH ME
   1. Secret Flight...65
   2. Taming a Texan..69
   3. Troubled Intruder..73
   4. Catshot...79
   5. Night Work 83
   6. Moonless Night...89
   7. Low Fuel..93
   8. Getting Arrested..97

III. EMOTIONS
   1. Safe Home 103
   2. April First...107
   3. Turning Sixty 111
   4. Crisis Struck 115

5. Chain Reaction 119
6. Missed Me 123
7. There was a Time...127
8. Now What...131
9. Will it Work 135

IV. MILITARY LIFE
1. Naval Academy...141
2. Reservist in Service 145
3. A Calling...153
4. Hitting Bottom..159

V. POTPOURRI
1. Maiden Voyages..165
2. Near Career..169
3. Pet Love 173

ACKNOWLEDGEMENTS

As it seems to be with writing and self-publishing a book of memoirs, there are many kind folks along the way who inspire, assist, listen and encourage. *That's How I Remember It,* is no exception. Credit for the quality of my writings goes out to a vast number and I take this opportunity to recognize them. I much appreciate each one of my friends and colleagues who have helped keep me on track as the book has come together. You know who you are and I am grateful to each of you.

As I did in my previous book, *Memories of Estelline,* I hereby acknowledge Rosalind (Roz) Kamholtz, Setauket, New York, for getting me started on my journey of memoir writing, ten years ago. Her strong leadership would not let me quit or fail. Due to her ill health, we've lost the writing liaison we once had. I wish her all the very best, I thank her, and I do miss her professionalism as a journalist advisor. Her Round Table, Memoir Writing workshop, at Stony Brook University, caught my attention in 1998 and from there I became an author.

Now retired journalism experts, Blake Kellogg, Madison, Wisconsin, and Del Harding, Windsor, Colorado, both long-time friends from the 1950s, have been certain and reliable help as they so willingly "eyeballed" my writings with their red pens charged.

The Estelline Journal, Estelline, South Dakota, a classic and enduring weekly newspaper from my old hometown, has so kindly published half of the stories in this book, over the past three years. In so doing, Publishers Greg and LeeAnne Archer have earned my sincere appreciation.

Chuck Cecil, South Dakota Author, Brookings, South Dakota, encouraged me to write this, my second book, with this enthusiasm and ideas. He, again, has willingly written the blurb on the back cover, as he did on *Memories of Estelline,* published in 2006. Chuck has served in the Navy and is a fellow graduate of South Dakota State College (now University).

Harvey Donley, owner of the Hoffelt Drugstore Museum, Estelline, South Dakota earns thanks for use of photography from his collection.

Many dedicated, accomplished and helpful colleagues in writing workshops from Osher Lifelong Learning Institute (OLLI) at Stony Brook University, New York, deserve sincere thanks for constructive criticism and input received over the years we have enjoyed working together learning to write right!

Sincere and grateful thanks go to OLLI workshop leaders, Sheila Bieber, Dorothy Schiff Shannon, and John Williams for their attention to detail in keeping workshop members on task and producing good works.

Lastly, I wish to acknowledge the many readers who have given written feedback on, *Memories of Estelline*. Their thoughts and opinions have been invaluable and most appreciated. They have given me the courage and motivation to publish, *That's How I Remember It*. Here is my best effort to do just that — I hope you find it worthy and enjoyable.

INTRODUCTION

That's How I Remember It, my second book of memoirs, is coming your way for good and worthwhile reasons. Writing and self-publishing is stimulating, it permits me to excitingly relive those special times you hear my writing voice telling you about. Those faces from the past, dates, times and details come back as if they are happening all over again. If you should ever feel like taking pen in hand and reminiscing a bit, you will see what I mean. In some instances, I recall sad or nerve-shattering situations that some years back taught me a lesson. Stories with sadness and loss allow me to bring back to life, for the moment, a loved one, dear family member or friend. You cannot imagine the recollections you have stored in your mind until you call upon them to reappear, by writing a memoir.

In this book, I continue my first journalistic attempt, *Memories of Estelline.* My indelible and fond hometown memories, of Estelline, South Dakota, never cease to live within me. I hope my stories bring back good and similar recollections for you. Being one of the chosen few who have had the opportunity and privilege to grow up in an eastern South Dakota farming community, in the 1930s and 1940s, I remain a proud and dedicated South Dakotan. I attended kindergarten through high school, with hometown friends and graduated mid-century with the EHS Class of 1950. The nineteen members of my graduating class treated each other like family, as did the other schoolmates in the classes before and after us at Estelline High School, enrollment 90. Many of us remain close friends nearly 60 years after leaving Estelline to seek our fortunes. My thirteen growing-up years in Estelline's schoolhouse were formative; they had a great deal to do with shaping who I am today, at age 77.

My return visits to Estelline bring back heartfelt memories of how the town was all for one and one for all; that's how we lived. No one locked the doors to their homes and car keys stayed in the car. Arguments were few and short-lived; folks were law-abiding. People understood that we were only as well-off as the folks around us. In Estelline peace reigned. I have returned for a visit nearly every year since I retired in 1996. It's a good feeling to return home. Estelline people don't change as they are still caring and progressive in their thinking.

My stories go beyond the city limits of my hometown, telling of successes and failures beyond. I have had numerous additional levels of personal development along life's way, but this "young raw Roth kid" was originally piece together in Estelline. Stories within these hard covers include a mix of days spent at United States Naval Academy, attending South Dakota State College, serving as a naval reservist, learning to fly Navy, flying from aircraft carriers, in air combat, flight testing, raising a family as a single-parent, re-marrying to start again, critical health situations and other good times told.

Readers may note occasional minor repeats of information from story to story. It is difficult to avoid duplication when the telling of stories and situations sometimes overlap. My stories are written at different times and in different moods. Attempting to avoid occasional retelling of parts of a story previously told was one of the difficulties encounter in creating this book.

It is my pleasure to have your attention and I hope I can entertain you for awhile with the telling of these bits and pieces of what life has done with and for me. Let me know what you think, I appreciate your feedback.

E-S-T-E-L-L-I-N-E

SATURDAY NIGHTS

No doubt about it — *Saturday Nights* were the greatest! Everyone, farm families and city dwellers alike, loved the excitement and camaraderie of this, the biggest night of the week. It was a warm and festive-type atmosphere in Estelline, South Dakota, by necessity and tradition. "Country kids" and their parents came to town for their needs, both material and social. Local merchants enjoyed the crowds that energized the ringing of their cash registers. Farmers marketed their produce, purchased groceries and dry goods, and then would spent their free time chatting, eating, drinking, bowling, movie-going and socializing. The City of Estelline's population grew from 600 to 1,500+ on *Saturday Nights*. Cars jammed Main Street, parked at all angles, while drivers vied for good spots, which were always at a premium.

The farm family routine, on Saturday, consisted of getting chores done as early as possible and ensuring that all had their "full bath" and were dressed in "going-to-town" clothes. Everyone squeezed into the family sedan, with no room to spare, eggs and cream cans in the trunk and occasionally a crate of chickens for market mounted on the sedan's roof top. Money from sale of produce paid for the store-bought things that returned home in the car trunk. The business of trading and shopping was done by parents, while kids connected with their friends for some fun, on this, the only time some friends were able to see each other during summer vacation from school.

Moms met with other moms to share news and gossip. Dads connected with other dads for some beers and conversation. Young sweethearts strolled along together looking for needed privacy to express their affection.

A parade of cars continued up and down Main Street all evening, with drivers showing off the newness and beauty of their "buggies." Children played and darted in between parked cars while moms showed concern for the little ones' whereabouts and safety. There was chaos and confusion at times, but it was all part of the ritual. Parents found it difficult to control their children with so much activity and excitement going on in all directions.

Chemical and Ladder trucks are fire apparatus used by Estelline Volunteer Fire Company in 1930s and early 1940s.

Popcorn street-vendors kept the scent of fresh-popped corn floating through the evening air to promote sales. The local movie house ran an early and a late show to accommodate the overflow of patrons. The pool hall had hot billiard competitions to watch; the line waiting to participate was long. Church and other organizations held street sales of homemade cupcakes and goodies to help fundraising for their causes. The duck-pin alley, downstairs at Gambles, had standing room only and best of all was the great "people watching" up and down Main Street, all evening at no charge.

There was order amid the bustle. People seemed to get along. Estelline had no patrols for law enforcement — none seemed necessary. Folks behaved and policed themselves. Certain ones sometimes over-drank their limit and an occasional outburst of profanity might break tranquility, but usually peace reigned.

On one of those *Saturday Nights* I remember best, the town's fire whistle sounded, about nine o'clock, with things running at the usual — full pitch! The Estelline Volunteer Fire Department was logically made up of the businessmen from Main Street. Shopping and activity seemed to freeze in place as men in aprons and business-wear dashed, from their shops, to the firehouse to man the apparatus. Fire trucks rolled with some folks following in cars, curious to know what was burning. Very shortly after they had departed, the trucks and firemen returned — a car fire had erupted a mile or so east of town and was extinguished as quickly as it had begun. *Saturday Night* resumed, as if nothing had happened. Everyone picked up their scripts on queue.

The regular conversations on the street were the main form of communications in the 1930s and '40s. If you didn't hear the news there, you probably weren't going to hear it at all! People sat at the curb, in parked cars with windows rolled down, hoping friends and acquaintances would stop to chat. "The word" got around amazingly well, whether it was believable, or not, was yet another matter. Excitement, action and fun lasted from early evening until near midnight when Main Street became deserted once again and the city's sidewalks seemed to *roll-up* for another night.

On Sunday, church people reviewed what they had heard, seen and done while in town the night before. A week would pass until *Saturday Night* "fever" happened again — in Estelline. If, due to illness, hardship, or because of something-or-other you missed it, there were no "make ups."

Then things changed. Television, multi-plex theatres, improved roads, better cars, bigger towns with more competitive prices, and the loss of loyalty to hometown merchants, began to ruin the good times in Estelline. Over time, the tradition died. Those who can recall, still miss — *Saturday Nights* in Estelline!

That's how I remember it.

FARMER JACK

It was a big farm in the eyes of this young lad; there were things happening all over the place. Farmer Jack's life style was "country living," on his farm near the southwest city limit of Estelline, South Dakota. I had an obsession — it was spending time with him whenever I could. On days when our parents needed help with child care, Bill, my older brother, and I spent time there being looked after by Jack's conscientious daughter, Eva Jane. She kept us overnight occasionally; those were sleepovers to remember. Jack's farm was "top of the line," by 1938 standards, and close enough that we could walk to it from our home in town.

Two large red barns served as the center piece for Jack's spread. The farm house was dwarfed by the barns, but it had many bedrooms. There were numerous other structures on the property including a chicken coop, pig shed, machinery shelter, grain storage bin, silo, pump-house, garage, three-hole outhouse, and a unique but smaller round barn. While pointing and joking, Jack explained, "Some folks go plum crazy in there, hunting for a corner to pee." Being on the farm for the day was like heaven. I loved all the excitement and unusual things that went on - even on Sundays.

Jack was a jolly fellow with a huge smile and no teeth. He enjoyed playing tricks, surprising us and coming up with things we'd not seen, or done before. He trusted us with milking cows, feeding hogs, collecting eggs, and other farm-chore type things. He called us "city slickers," but he was only fooling. Jack wore a heavy tan and had a strong back capable of lifting, or moving, most anything. At meal time, he ate as if he hadn't had food for days. Blessings at the family dinner table were always said by Jack and it was from him the family took their cues and orders.

Jack called his wife "The Mrs." — they had a number of kids. "Mrs. Jack" spent long hours, in the kitchen, processing milk and cream, preparing meals and baking goodies of all kinds. Farmers ate well and often to keep their energy up. Work seemed endless as there was always a chore left to be done. I was "Jimmie Boy," my brother was called "Billie Boy." Jack always had a nick-name for everyone. I, no doubt, was his favorite because I followed him everywhere. I did my best to avoid being a pain in his butt.

Amazingly, Jack always knew just what to do next — he had instincts and an agenda with ample know-how to carry them out.

Occasionally, usually on a Saturday night, barn dances were held in the largest of Farmer Jack's barns. Colorful, handmade dance bills were placed in stores around town announcing the date and time of these fun gatherings. Farm and city folks arrived by the carload so good parking was at a premium. Few fun-lovers missed the chance to come have some excitement in Jack's hay loft. He told us all about those "follies," but we felt he sometimes left out many details. We heard tales told around town about barn dance behavior, but we never knew for certain how much was the truth. Our young minds could only imagine the shenanigans that went on in that hay loft. It befuddled us trying to envision ladies and gents scampering up and down vertical wooden ladders — the only way to come and go to a barn dance. We felt certain that ladies weren't wearing party dresses! Under age children were not allowed in the area on dance nights — we were miffed that no one would tell us how much older we must grow to "be of age." Spying on a barn dance was something we discussed, but the occasion never presented itself. Hot summer nights, with kegs of beer, bottles of whiskey and musicians with drums, fiddles, accordions, trumpets, guitars, banjos and loud singers juiced up the crowd. People danced until they dropped. We knew that much was true and we wondered what the milk cows were thinking down below while the ruckus reigned, throughout the night, topside.

During milk chore time, I tried repeatedly, yanking and squeezing on the cow udder's protuberance in an attempt to get milk flowing into the bucket, but I didn't seem to have the touch. I did help carry filled milk buckets to the farm house where separating took place. Milk was poured into tanks and the process began by cranking the large wooden handle. Cream was separated from the milk as cranking went on, and on, and on. It was fun for awhile, but usually an adult took over to speed things up. Milk was processed twice per day, every day. Cows knew no holidays; milking the herd was a major chore. Cans of cream and milk were transported to the Estelline Creamery, for market and storage on large blocks of ice.

Collecting eggs in the hen house was much easier than milking. Fetching eggs from the nests was more fun than the hunt for colored eggs on Easter morning as Jack's brood left their shelled treasures in plain view. Clucking loudly, the hens seemed happy and proud of what they had produced. The roosters roaming about were usually ornery as heck — we dodged and weaved to avoid their pecks and scratches. Spending an overnight on Jack's farm was a momentous occasion, a rare treat it was. A big farmer breakfast was assured in the morning with fresh eggs, bacon and milk. We were oblivious to the fact that strips of bacon on our plates were most likely harvested from slaughtered piglets we'd recently wrestled with and hand fed in Jack's pig yard.

Not an everyday chore, but an important one, was cleaning the cow stalls and spreading the manure in the fields; it was a tough job with a strong odor. Horses pulled the spreader and didn't seem to mind the smell. They knew the route and seldom got bogged down in the muck. City slickers, Jimmie-Boy and Billie-Boy, were coaxed to the barns to help shovel manure from the stalls into the spreader, but we kept our distance, preferring to watch. Pitching clean straw into the stalls with a man-size pitch fork, was lighter work, but we didn't last long at that either. Spending time on the farm helped Bill and me to better understand why farm guys reeked of manure when they came to town wearing their ripe coveralls and boots. Keeping clothes unsoiled, while doing messy farm chores compared well with attempting to nail jell-o to the wall. I soiled my clothes one time when I tumbled while chasing a new-born calf in the pasture. Landing full force in the middle of a huge cow pie; I was a mess. Checking out for the day, I headed home to clean up and change clothes. My "cow pie tumble" was a favorite of Jack's for his story-telling.

A shiny red tractor was one of Jack's favorite farm implements and mine too. Horses customarily did the hauling and pulling, but tractors were becoming more popular as they required less care and feeding. One day, around July 4th, the date sticks with me as corn was reaching knee high, Jack insisted I come with him to cultivate corn. I was a bit leery — this was something new to me.

He yelled, "Come along, Jimmie Boy, sit on my lap, I'll show you what to do."

I cautiously crawled up and plopped down, grabbing the steering wheel tightly with my undersized hands. Jack knew how much I loved to ride. When we got to the field, just south of the barns, he steered into rows of beautifully sprouting corn. Our mission was to clear the weeds that were invading the crop. I knew that much about farming. With both of us crowdedly sitting on an over-sized steel tractor seat, Jack gripped my slim and trim little body, snuggled in his lap. I was quite comfortable. After a time, he surprisingly turned steering over to me. I was shocked that he trusted me with such an important job. His hand lightly guided my steering, at first. Then he stuck his hand in his pocket and told me I could handle things by myself. In my exuberance, I became a bit rambunctious as we moved along and began to whip the steering wheel back and forth from side to side causing the cultivator blades to dig up corn plants unmercifully. Jack grabbed back control, while laughing so hard he was temporarily blinded by tears. I was frightened — thinking of how badly I had damaged the stalks of corn I'd just plowed under by mistake. He thought the ordeal was hilarious, but kept tight control of things from that point. Later, while returning to the yard, he allowed to me steer again as he sang, "I wish I had my belly full of beer." Jack knew Dad owned a beer hall in town. He truly enjoyed going there to tip a few on occasion. Dropping by Roth's Recreation Parlor for a beer break revved-up the day for many farm hands. Numbers of times thereafter, much to my embarrassment, Jack told about the day I had clobbered his corn with the cultivator.

Harvest time came at summer's end; it was a busy and exciting time. Farm neighbors generally worked well together sharing chores and heavy work loads. In late August and September, all hands turned to for the small grain harvest, it was a social experience as well as dawn to dusk workdays. When the huge thrashing machine was towed to Jack's place, the fun began. Farmers with their wives, sons and daughters came en masse by car, truck, tractor and horse drawn wagon to load and deliver the grain bundles to the thrasher (they called it pitching bundles), and to help deliver grain to elevators in town where the bounty was weighed, sold and shipped out by rail. It was a time to celebrate the success of the growing season. Money began its flow back into the farmers' bank accounts! Harvest time had a "circus atmosphere"' — there were so many things happening. Wives, daughters and girlfriends worked together, day long, to provide delicious home-cooked food for everyone. It seemed like work stopped every three to four hours for the crew to eat again. This thrashing routine lasted as many days as it took until all had their fields harvested. Fortunately, when thrashing at Jack's place was finished, the Roth brothers went back into town to pick up their city-slicker routine.

Those special times when we were allowed to sleep over at Jack's were interesting; we learned about life with limited facilities. Using the outhouse was spooky even with flashlights to illuminate the operation. Kerosene lamps stood filled and ready in case of power failure; which seemed to happen quite often. Jack taught us about farm safety; fire prevention was always on his mind. Barn fires raged quickly once they started and rarely was a barn spared. Smoking was never permitted near the barns. We wondered if the rule held up on barn dance nights.

The location where Jack's farm once stood so majestically has changed — the buildings are long gone. Estelline's municipal airport was built on the acreage in the late 1940's; two intersecting grass airstrips, night landing lights, aviation fuel and limited flight line service were available. Used sparingly, by the chosen few, it eventually closed and land was returned to agriculture. Today, the Country Corner Convenience store, with its fuel pumps, rental storage units, car and truck wash and snack bar, sits near where barn dancing once reigned. If Jack were still with us he would love the convenience store with its refrigerated coolers full of domestic and imported beer, placed in the spot where his farm house once stood.

That's how I remember it.

Jim and Bill Roth <u>stand at attention</u> on a play day while living in the Sonnenburg House on 6th Street in Estelline, it was Fall of 1937.

STRANGER IN TOWN

Tall, thin and full-bearded, with long bushy hair, looking as though it had yet to experience the treat of shears, the man was strange looking. Wearing his signature floppy, crusty old boots; his walk was slow and deliberate. A shabby top hat, unusual for the times, touched off his always rumpled bib overalls and shirt. A mix of body odor and the scent of horse manure announced his presence; you could count on it. As young pals, I and my gang spent our time looking to find something new or different, to liven up our day. This stranger in Estelline captivated our interest.

Sightings were seldom, but when "the stranger" did appear, we dropped whatever we were doing for another close-up view. He preferred that we keep our distance and we usually did. Seldom did he look anyone in the eye; he rarely spoke a word. If anyone tried to get close, he'd stare that person down with his dark beady eyes, as if daring the individual to open his mouth. "Ole Slow" was the handle we attached to the guy and we never did hear him called by another. He showed true affection for his sway-backed horse. It was black like his hat and was stabled in a derelict shed behind Ole's humble quarters. The horse was old; we could tell. It was difficult to guess Ole's age. His pace was slow, as was the speed of the buggy his horse pulled on rare occasions when the two of them paraded through town.

The old rickety building where Ole lived was once a school house — so we were told. It was located at the north end of Estelline's two-block long business district, on the west side of Main Street, across from the Standard Oil Station. It was an awfully ugly building to be located so prominently, in the center of town. Exterior paint had long ago deteriorated; the wood siding was in disrepair. A sagging roof and missing window panes seemed a match for the leaning brick chimney that defied gravity as it survived year after year. In the rear of the property was a dilapidated shed with just room enough to accommodate an old horse and its frayed and wobbly buggy. Seldom seen in motion, Ole, his horse and the buggy were a "show-stopper" when they appeared. The sight was "talk of the town" for kids; even adults stopped to gawk. By the early 1940s, cars had pretty much taken over transportation. Horses seldom came into town; rather they stayed on the farm to help work the fields.

Ole seemed to have no friends, or people to talk to; he was a loner. The horse provided his only companionship, as far as we could tell. Ole slowly climbed the exposed staircase on the south side of the building when heading for his quarters on the second floor. We didn't see lights on at night, or smoke coming from the chimney when it was cold. One could only imagine the conditions under which he lived. The place we saw him most often was in the shed area tending to his horse. *Where and when did he shop for food and other needs including feed for his horse?* We wondered. Ole seemed to live his life avoiding people. There was speculation as to what he did for entertainment and if he could read or write. *How did he get his money, mail and other necessary things? What did he do when he took ill?* There were just so many questions about Ole — he kept us mystified. We wanted to get to know him better and perhaps to help him, if we could. Not one of us seemed to have the courage to approach the man in a warm and friendly manner. I guess it was because we were just kids and he seemed so unfriendly toward us.

Our parents warned us, "Stay away from Ole Slow!" His actions and appearance were strange; parents were uncertain as to what he might do. The caution just added intrigue to our "kid-fixation" with this unusual person. Often, there were dares in our play, from standing under the railroad bridge as the freight train passed to diving from high atop Murphy's Bridge into the murky waters of the Big Sioux River, a mile west of town. It happened as simple as can be one dark evening when Estelline was all quiet and nothing was happening to entertain us. A dare to climb Ole's staircase for a peek into his quarters was offered up in fun. Before anyone spoke, I took the challenge. After mustering my courage, I crept slowly toward the staircase. Believing darkness would be good cover, my foot hit the first of about twenty creaky old steps. With certainty that I could carry out the mission, I climbed, gaining courage step by step. As I neared the top, with a breast full of pride, the quiet of the night was shattered by the wailing scream of the town's fire siren, located just one block away. It was 9:00 p.m! One long blast signified time for kids below age 16 to be off the streets — it was our curfew. Knowing the city night watchman would soon be on patrol, my buddies left me "hanging" as they beat it for home. With the beejeebers scared out of me, I stood frozen. It took less than a second to abandon my plan and to scamper down the staircase racing for home. The two-block sprint took just seconds. I stepped inside and slammed the back door, feeling relief. *No kid ever got closer to seeing Ole's quarters,* I told my ten-year-old self, as I slipped into a clean and dry set of drawers.

Time passed and our interest in getting a peek inside Ole's place seemed to wane. One night a fire broke out in the old building. Someone noted smoke and flames appearing from the upper area where Ole lived. Central operator, at the telephone office, was alerted to sound the fire alarm (the same siren used to signal our evening curfew.) Local fire department volunteers scrambled quickly, dousing the flames and carrying Ole to safety. We were in bed as it was late, so we missed what must have been an eerie scene. The next day, when we heard, our minds were filled with questions; our hearts were filled with concern. The building received little apparent damage. Ole was admitted to the local hospital for care. The thought of the staff having to clean him up and treat his burns and injuries was disconcerting, and we had additional concerns. *Who would tend to Ole's horse? Could we now climb the staircase to sneak a peek at Ole's quarters?* No one seemed interested in doing so; we were more concerned about Ole's health and his future. Word wasn't forthcoming in the community about his condition. There was no sign of life around the property where Ole and his horse had been such fixtures. Eventually we realized the horse was gone — either dead, or moved by some good person to a better place.

Word finally came out that Ole was dead. He was unable to recover from smoke inhalation and serious burns from the fire. When the news leaked out that Ole's life had ended, that was it. We never heard another word about Ole Slow, his horse, if a service was held, or where the two of them may have been buried. Strange looking Ole and his old black horse had become part of us. We felt sadness...we missed having "a stranger in town" with his trusty old steed.

That's how I remember it.

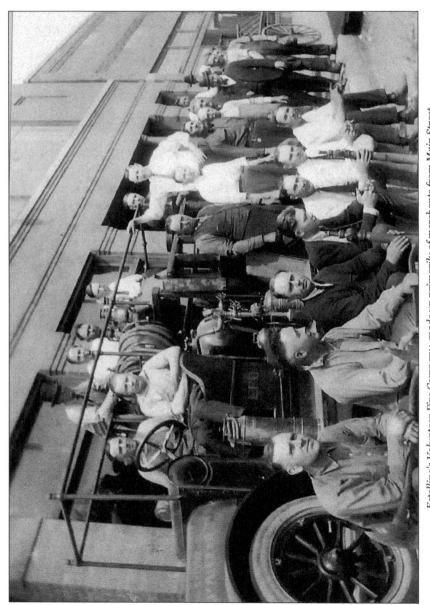

Estelline's Volunteer Fire Company, made up primarily of merchants from Main Street, sit at the ready for the fire whistle to blow.

UNIFORM OF THE DAY

It was her signal; we knew it well. There was no doubt; Mom's day had begun. When she pulled it off the hook and flipped the loop around her neck, tying the strings behind her as she trotted about, we knew her day was off and running. It was her work-apron, her uniform-of-the-day; it stayed in place from early morning until after the evening meal. When she finally retired it, back on the hook, or in the dirty clothes hamper — it was her subtle announcement that her work day was about over.

She learned the many applications of an apron from her mother before her. It was Mom's most useful housekeeping tool. In the pockets, she stowed things that perhaps could be useful to someone during the course of her day. A dust cloth, band-aid, handkerchief, note pad, pencil, toothpick, safety pin, small screwdriver, nail clipper...were some things usually found on board. Miscellaneous items were carried, in apron pockets, to save her footsteps throughout the day. She had plain aprons, flowery aprons, long aprons, short aprons and holiday aprons — a supply for all occasions.

Mom chased the dust, dried her hands, wiped away tears, stopped the bleeding, cleaned her eye-glasses, held hot pan handles, opened tough jars, carried the laundry, gathered loose stuff scattered about, with her apron... just for starters. It protected the clothing she was wearing, but that wasn't the major reason she always donned her apron. She would wrap the apron around her arms when she was cold; she'd wipe perspiration from her brow when she'd worked up a sweat. Mom was seldom seen, about our home, without her "uniform of the day."

Aprons were not only worn by moms at home, they were common place throughout the Fair City of Estelline. Joe, the shoemaker, was never without his apron; Butcher Blote paraded through his market, and out on Main, in his long white, blood-spattered apron. Dad wore his work apron while tending bar and serving snacks in his pool hall. Smitty wore a short-folded apron behind the counter in his café to ward off food spills while mechanics at Fasbender and Eisnach Garage protected their clothes from oil, grease and dirt with leather aprons. Blacksmith Kalsbeck protected his body from heat, sparks and flying embers by use of an asbestos apron. Aprons covered with flour, jelly and crumbs, were standard garb at

Baker's Bakery. Counter clerks, Chuck Leighton and Buck Zebell, at Davis and White Company, hustled about in long white aprons, fetching grocery items for customers. When entering a place of business, you could tell who the "players" were by the aprons they wore. The day I assumed command of the shiny chrome Birch popcorn machine at State Theatre, I was dressed in a somewhat over-sized, full-length, white apron with pockets and high-lighted by long tie-strings flopping in the rear. When I first donned the ugly thing I felt a bit weird, but in time, I wore it with the same pride that a cop wears his badge.

Wearing an apron sure seems to have lost its appeal over the years. I'm not certain why. Perhaps it's to save some time — by not having to find it, put it on and stow it properly after the job is done. Plain, fancy, long, short, humorous, patriotic and other theme aprons are frequently given as gifts. They get stashed in a cupboard drawer, or hung on a hook in the pantry, but you seldom see them in action. I have serious doubt there will ever be anything discovered to replace this once popular item. How could something, once so common and useful, disappear from holiday gift lists and end up abandoned in the bottom of a drawer, sort of disappointedly, to become no longer the uniform-of-the-day?

That's how I remember it.

THE ROTH HOUSE

"Oh, what stories could be told, if only the house could speak." Built in the early days of a festering World War II, the contractor ran out of building materials so finishing touches had to wait until after the war ended. From its beginning, it was attractive with considerable potential. It was said to be one of the most admired houses in our town. Due to the existing housing shortage in Estelline, the first occupants accepted the house by renting "as is."

Les and Cathryn Roth, my parents, were the second family to call the Dutch Colonial house their home. At 307 - 5th Street North, in Estelline, South Dakota, it was the first and only house my parents ever owned. Our occupancy lasted four decades, 1945 to 1984. Those were the most impressionable years of our lives. When Mom and Dad sold and moved to Phoenix, Arizona, their departure wasn't easy. They struggled to say "farewell" to a house and a town that were chock full of wonderful memories.

Three families subsequently called the house their home. An Air Force officer's widow moved from Rapid City, after deciding to purchase rather quickly. Since my deceased brother had been career Air Force, it pleased my parents to see her as the home's new owner. In that she was new to the community and with no kids, neighbors saw her signature as two dogs penned in the back yard with a doghouse centerpiece. Listening to barking dogs was change for the neighborhood. After a rather short residency, she, surprisingly, sold and left town before her roots had enough time to develop.

The Derby family arrived, as the next owners. Their three young daughters grew and so did their need for more living space. A walkout deck was added, the detached garage was expanded and a basketball court appeared in the driveway. Eventually they sold and moved to a larger newly-built house nearby.

The Wegners purchased the house, becoming the fifth family to call it home. They set about raising a family, while taking-on numerous home improvements, both inside and out. Seven layers of wallpaper had to be removed in order to paint the walls. The roof was replaced, and a fresh coat of paint was applied to the exterior. The fluttering *Old Glory* and lamp post out front gave the same look established by the Roths years before.

* * * * *

When our family first arrived in Estelline, in 1934, we lived in a rental house, south of Highway 28. Bill was four-years-old, I was two, and this was the first house that I remember. When Dad started his business, on Main Street, he was the youngest businessman in town, at age 22. In less than a year, we upgraded to a better house next to the city's ball parks and where an ice skating rink appeared in winter. The *Sonnenburg House,* as it was known in Estelline, named after the original owners, was in a neighborhood loaded with kids. Play went on full time and we enjoyed the open spaces across the street. From there, we could hear Mom yelling, for us, when we needed to come home. It was as if we were playing in an extended back yard.

In 1940, a logistic crisis developed. Another move became necessary when the Sonnenburgs suddenly sold "out from under us." We had been paying rent checks faithfully, while waiting for the house to go on the market. The owners foiled us by selling to another party. The Roth brothers, not yet in their teens, learned the fateful news by accidentally overhearing adult conversation. Things looked grim, as there were no unoccupied homes available in town to rent or buy. Building anew was out of the question, due to building material shortages. With no place to go, we contemplated having to leave town. That would not have been a good thing. I shudder to think how so doing would have changed my life.

Dad and Mom were deeply concerned, but soon conceived of a "lifesaving" idea. There would be hardships, but nevertheless we decided, one way, or another, we could work things out. The good news was we wouldn't be leaving Estelline! Dad was able to work out an arrangement that most folks thought impossible. Widow Lohr (Mrs. Annie), who had moved upstairs to an apartment over her drugstore on Main Street after her husband died, agreed to rent her "boarded-over" farm house. Our family promised to help Mrs. Lohr with her relocation in every way possible.

Located on the northwest corner of Estelline, the Lohr property consisted of a modest unoccupied house, big red barn, deluxe privy with multiple stations, and seven spacious acres with a large cottonwood grove and rolling hills and pasture. The Chicago and Northwestern Railroad tracks ran alongside the west boundary. "How exciting it was going to be watching passing freight trains," we thought. Our minds were busy contemplating challenges and unknowns that would certainly arise in these, our new, surroundings.

We began work by opening doors and windows boarded over for protection. A "haunted house" scene was revealed as the interior of the house was layered with dust and cobwebs. We stood in silence and stared, realizing the drastic changes in life style we were going to be dealing with here. After hauling, lugging and storing Annie Lohr's furnishings in a secured section of the barn, we set about overhauling the interior of the house — cleaning, painting and wallpapering.

Further investigation revealed the house had few amenities: no state-of-the-art plumbing, few electrical outlets and an out-dated coal-burning furnace. Most of the windows were stuck shut from layers of old paint and deterioration. The first days onboard were similar to roughing it at YMCA Camp.

We committed to life "on the farm" for several years, until war ended. In time, we adjusted to the inescapable cold of winter, the dark and lonely treks to the outhouse, bathing in a wash tub and the one lone cold water tap mounted in the kitchen. We prayed the old cesspool where the kitchen sink drained wouldn't collapse. Wearing extra clothing and piling heavy quilts on the beds helped us to endure the cold. It was impossible for the antiquated coal furnace, in the basement, to manage adequate heat at times when temperatures were sub-zero. The house was seldom comfy. We had hot in summer and cold in winter, no matter what. Complaining to the owner was foolish in that we had practically forced our way in. Instead, we did our best to work things out and to live in harmony while awaiting better times.

Good news arrived on my thirteenth birthday, much to our delight. It meant — not another winter on the farm! A new house in town, being rented by the Force family, became available in the fall of 1945. Dr. Ronald Force, the local dentist, had been called up for military service. His family decided to move out west to be near him. Upon departure, they left behind a house full of furnishings. The interior of the house was livable, but not finished due to material shortages. Dr. and Mrs. Force opted not to return to the house at war's end, as its size would no longer comfortably accommodate their growing family.

When the house was placed on the market, we quickly closed a deal. In short order, we moved in. The flush toilet, state-of-the-art heating system, non-creaky floors and functional windows were luxuries we enjoyed. The move into a partially unfinished house, at 307 - 5th Street North, was like "rising up to heaven." After years of enduring the elements, the outhouse, no bathroom, no plumbing, and a number of other unpleasantries, we felt blessed.

Improvements began, before the last pictures were hung. Once fixtures and materials became available, home projects seemed never-ending. Working evenings, removing old linoleum and installing hardwood flooring, became an entertainment project, for the whole family. Dad was the handy one who gave orders while teaching us to be good help. Home ownership seemed to energize all four of us. An oversize garage was built for the car and storage.

Eventually, we converted the coal furnace to propane gas and the coal bin became a shelved storage area. The kitchen remodeling impacted our daily routine the most as we had to eat meals out for a few days while new cabinets were installed, a breakfast nook was assembled, and appliances were replaced. Adding a toilet and shower in the basement eased the strain especially when we had visitors. The "frosting on the cake" came some years later when central air-conditioning was installed. The house was short on storage space from its beginning so when the A/C ductwork was placed in closets it enlarged the problem. In the end, the comfort we gained was worth the space lost.

More property was added, for gardening and recreation area, by purchasing a portion of the lot next to us. School was one block away and we enjoyed walking home for lunch. Dad could stroll two blocks to work, on Main Street. We liked our new location and in no time the house became our treasured home. Life was good.

* * * * * *

Fifty years after my departure, while on a return trip to Estelline for a school reunion, I took a drive around town. Passing 5th Street, I was drawn to our former house. The view brought back a flood of memories. After setting the brake, I leaped out with camera in hand. My heart was pounding as I approached the door. Angie Wegner answered my knock with her arms full of little children. After introductions, I asked if she'd mind me clicking a few photos.

"Please excuse the mess, we're doing some redecorating, but do come inside for a look. Take as many photos as you'd like," she said while casu-

The Roth House, Estelline, South Dakota,
is still looking good with its present owners, the Wegner Family.

ally escorting me and her little ones about the house. Peering into my old bedroom stopped me in my tracks.

"It may sound a bit strange, but I can't stop thinking of how things were when this was our home. Here's where I finished my growing-up years, enjoying Mom's great meals and her caring ways, and Dad's companionship and firm guidance. I took my first solo drive, in the family car, from the driveway, entertained my first serious girlfriend, in these quarters, laughed many times, cried real tears, and left for college, from the safety of this place." I reminisced, as she listened with interest.

"I fully understand. We quickly learned to love it here as well."

I kept going, *"Under this roof, our family shared many occasions. Some were happy times, while others were tough times. We learned how to sort them out together successfully. I best recall the fond memories."*

Then it was time to say goodbye. While thanking Angie and turning to leave, I felt a slight lump in my throat; a bit of a tear began its track down my cheek. I heard her final remark, one I will always remember.

In the back yard of The Roth House, celebrating Gram Lowthian's birthday with her eight grandchildren (L to R) David Lehrer, Jim Roth, Cathy Gailor, Midshipman Bill Roth, Frank Gailor, and the Hamilton girls, Carol, Dorothy and Mary, July 1951.

"*It won't matter how long our family lives here; this house will always be known in Estelline as "The Roth House."* I could tell she was sincere.

As I drove on down the street, one I had traveled many times before, a thought struck me. "*The Roth House symbolizes all that is left of the Roth family era in Estelline — Bill died in 1966, Dad in 1990 and Mom in 2004.*" I mind was awash with nostalgia. It had me in its grip.

That's how I remember it.

SNOWFALL

When the South Dakota weatherman "caused" a major snowfall, it changed things. Heavy snow slowed transportation to a crawl and brought hardships, but it meant fun and excitement for kids turned "snow-bunny." School closed, the train and mail bus cancelled service and church meetings were postponed. Business stopped. People stayed home to batten down the hatches until snowfall let up and the wind stopped its drift sculpturing.

Heavy winter snowfall sometimes customers close to home and away from stores for days. When business stopped, so did cash flow. In the 1930s and early 1940s, machinery for dealing with snow removal was scarce and slow moving. It was customary to see strong-backed men and boys, wielding shovels and grain scoops, clearing the way. Businessmen bundled up and left their shops to shovel out their walkways and parking areas, hoping to see customers returning to resume shopping, real soon.

Estelline was sometimes, jokingly, referred to as a "one-horse-town." Actually, it was the "biggest little town in South Dakota," with a population under 1,000. It boasted it own motorized grader for maintaining graveled roads and streets in the summer. The machine was county-owned however, and it did poorly moving snow in winter. Often stuck with wheels spinning and men pushing and digging to keep it moving, the grader was more of a nuisance in snow. Farm tractors with hydraulically operated manure bucket-loaders mounted up front, were the latest thing for barnyard cleanup. When the equipment was "enlisted" for snow removal, it was slow going. Moving large quantities of snow and clearing roads, by tractor, compared well with clearing your front steps with a teaspoon.

Tire chains were fitted on fire engines, tow trucks, ambulances and other emergency vehicles, but when snow was heavy and deep, vehicles got bogged down regardless. Driving with chains on the rear wheels was rough going. Vehicle transmissions, axles, rims and tires were not designed for such goings-on. If you had a trip you must take, a shovel was your best tool for making headway in heavy snow. There were snow tires available for purchase in winter. They were called "knobbies," because of their appearance and rough ride. The knobs were like teeth, biting into the snow. They helped some with getting traction in the heavy stuff, but their effectiveness was limited.

Radio weather forecasting was a bit of "guess work," less accurate than today, on television. Blizzards blew in, sometimes unexpectedly, with clear skies overhead and the sun, or moon in view. Visibility was reduced to near zero in dense blowing snow. The drifting snow quickly re-blocked roads that had been previously cleared. It was futile trying to keep roads open, until high winds subsided. Travel at night, and/or in sub-zero temperatures put lives at risk and was ill-advised. Challenging road conditions, with slippery surfaces layered with packed snow and ice, appeared as early as Halloween and could last until after Easter. Winter seemed the longest of the four seasons —and it was.

There were no major highways in and around Estelline. The eastern extreme of County Highway 28, an unimproved gravel road, was the main thoroughfare into town. Snow removal from residential streets was done by a small-size city work force, assisted by volunteers who were local residents and farmers. The hefty county snow plow usually arrived to help after the vast majority of the work was finished, as Estelline was located on the far eastern border of Hamlin County.

One farm family helped another and when chores were finished, some "work-horse" farmers walked into town to help get things up and running

*Snow removal was a problem after heavy
snowfall on Main Street, Estelline, South Dakota, about 1940.*

on Main Street. Hard-working snow scoopers could always count on a gratis lunch and a few free beers! Big storms created long days of hard manual labor. Volunteers turned such occasions into impromptu "snow festivals" with shoveling, talking, eating, drinking and more shoveling. Snow-clearing became a community affair, more of a social function, although no reigning royalty was ever chosen.

Homes were well stocked with food, for the long months of winter, so as not to get caught short. Keeping an abundant supply of coal, oil or wood, whichever was the fuel of choice, was prudent. Telephone service was occasionally lost during storms when contact was out due to high winds. The electrical power lines were also at risk of damage. Kerosene lamps and battery powered lights stood ready, as backup. Home heating systems were unsophisticated and could fight off cold only for as long as the fuel supply lasted.

Planned activities frequently got changed, in winter, due to weather. Schedules were flexible and events routinely had snow-day backup dates established in case of postponements. South Dakotans were raised to take the weather in stride. Accommodating weddings, funerals and the arrival of babies during winter months sometimes became tricky. Farmers were committed to feeding, watering and milking chores for the livestock, no matter what. The census showed few sissies lived in these parts, and many babies were born following tough winters, come September, October and November.

Some of the fun of winter was time spent with family on days when all were in "locked down" together due to snowfall. We enjoyed special meals, board games and entertaining ourselves, while waiting for the storm to subside. The television, personal computer, cell phone, ipod, Walkman, and electronic games were not yet available on shelves in stores. "Best Buy" was when your Mom purchased you a whole new outfit for $1.99 at a sale in the local dry goods store. Some used the phone lines for entertaining "chit-chat," but at our house the phone was for business, or emergencies —never for pleasure. Holding down the phone bill was everyone's job. It was Dad's rule—snow or no snow. Our telephone bill was based on measured minutes used and the cost for long distance calls was sky high.

Once when I was twelve-years-old, an unexpected snow storm blow in quickly. It was a whooper, which caught people off guard. The afternoon school bus return-run was cancelled for safety reasons. The country kids were stranded in town and places for them to stay-over had to be arranged.

We took in a "snow orphan" and his stay with us lasted for several days. Tommy was our age so the Roth brothers gained a live-in playmate. We loaned him pajamas, a toothbrush and clothes. Unfortunately, the phone lines were dead, damaged by the high winds, before Tommy's parents could be notified. They had to trust the school's emergency "buddy system," as they waited out the storm. Since there was no extra bed for Tommy, the three of us slept together on the floor. There were many snowfall-induced slumber parties as town folks shared homes for a few days and nights with a bus load of stranded country kids.

Snowfall continued relentlessly and we cheered it on. Strong winds whipped and swirled fluffy powder into high banks in all sizes and shapes. Some of the snow became a grainy mix as it blew through open farm fields picking up topsoil. High drifts were packed with a hard crust firm enough to support humans. We walked tall, looking down on our masterfully built snow caves and forts that had taken many hours to create. Tommy enjoyed playing with his new "brothers." He was happy to be missing out on his farm chores each morning and night. Living life as a "city slicker" seemed quite agreeable to him.

After nearly three straight days of on and off snowfall, skies cleared and sun light blazed brightly, but the frosty temperatures remained bitterly cold. The deep layers and drifts of snow had drastically changed the look of things. A gigantic bank of snow had formed, running the length of Main Street, blocking all traffic, even walkers. After climbing to the top of the snow "mountain" on Main, we were able to see the rooftops of stores. Second story windows were at eye level. It seemed very weird, like being in a wonderland.

Tommy's parents finally made it to town, after the county snow plow opened Highway 28, east of town. They came to rescue him after his three-night sleepover at our house. It was a happy reunion. School remained closed for five days, while we enjoyed winter sports—sledding, skiing, skating, snow fort building and snowball fighting.

Clearing the incredible amount of snow that blocked every street in town took time. Things did gradually return to normal, but temperatures remained well below freezing so the snow didn't go away. High piles from the shoveling were stacked everywhere; they made obstacles to be avoided. Fresh eggs, milk, bread and vegetables were slow in returning to shelves at the market. Mom kept us fed, on soup, crackers, canned fruits and vegetables, and pancakes. The local theatre was dark for eight days, until film delivery trucks were able to get their routes and deliveries back in order. It was standing-room-only when the first movie show ran following the storm. Patrons were happy to be back into their routine and mixing it up with other people once again. Post-storm business in Estelline was brisk. Story-telling seemed never-ending, as survivors told their snow tales. Some farm animals succumbed to the storm, but fortunately there were no human casualties in the area around Estelline.

A few more snowfalls visited that winter, but that "monster" stood alone. Grownups were happy with light to moderate stuff, while kids longed for one more really big one!

That's how I remember it.

NEED A HAIRCUT

I dreaded the thought and cringed when Mom started talking about the need for a haircut. We had two barbershops in Estelline. Few men and boys patronized both; each of us seemed to have our own favorite. The shops were located across the street from one another on Main Street. Ed Musolf was the haircutter on the east side. Bill Shnapp had his shop on the west side, three doors up from Roth's Recreation Parlor - known as The Pool Hall to most. I would stop at Dad's Parlor to see Dad and pick up some money before proceeding to my 'torture' in Bill's barber chair.

Early on, when I was a little kid, Mom would escort me to the barber. She always had her own definite specifications as to how my hair should look. Dislike was what I felt when going to the barber as I dreaded having hair clippings going up my nose and in my mouth. The worst part of the whole process was having Bill make me sit dead-still, to avoid the possibility of having my ear cut off. Bill never failed to give that caution, as I approached his chair. He embarrassed me by hoisting me up and placing my rump on a padded board placed across the armrests, disregarding my pleas to climb up by myself. Bill did this with his smaller patrons so as to place us at the correct height for his outstretched clippers. It seemed to take an hour, or more, to complete the whole ordeal. First was the combing, then came the watering down, followed by scissors, clippers and small talk. Bill's routine included frequent stops to chat a bit with other customers, or to stroll to the front window for a check on the action on Main — then more cutting, clipping and combing, before adding a dash of "dabble-do" from a jug to sweeten up the smell of my hair. He gave me no choice it was his show and my money going in the till.

Bill didn't always use his electric clippers, for some reason — I think it was so he could torture me with his hand-operated shears. As he clipped along, he would squeeze the handle grips on the clippers, back and forth, working his way up the back of my neck. When he pulled the clippers away, he'd sometimes catch a strand of hair still attached to my skin. I'd twitch and jump as it not only startled me...it hurt! In his efforts to hold my attention, Bill sometimes threatened to give me a shave with his straight edge razor. He'd grab the razor and stroke it on the large leather strap hanging from the back of his barber chair...to ensure it was razor sharp! I knew he was just "spoofing" with me, but I saw no humor at all in his antics.

When finished, Bill dumped a dash of talcum powder, on a long bristled brush, and swiped the loose hair from my face, neck and ears. His playful whisking tickled and he'd continue until I giggled or twitched — it was his typical finale. I knew I was free to escape the moment Bill removed the flowery drop cloth wrapped about me and as my shorn hair tumbled to the floor joining the other cuttings of the day.

Releasing a quarter from my sweaty palm — payment for the brutality — Bill would ring it up and drop it with a clank into the money drawer. I'd reach into a jar of lollypops, for my reward, while waiting for a friendly swat on my fanny. The barber shop ritual occurred every few weeks and the procedure never changed. As I grew older, I managed going for a haircut on my own, usually with strict instructions from Mom, beforehand. I would bribe Bill to fix me up with a crew-cut like most of the other kids wore. He'd never do it, having told Mom he couldn't as my hair was too fine and wouldn't stand up straight. I guess he cared about how I looked too.

Getting my hair cut turned critical one day when Bill closed his shop for retirement. I dreaded the thought of having to enter Ed's shop after my years of loyalty to Bill. After Mom denied my request for a ride to another town to get my hair cut, I had no other choice — Musolf's here I come! I didn't know quite how to face Ed. It wasn't as though I didn't know him; he was our neighbor and had a daughter, Vera, in my class. I thought he might refuse to do me, after all my years with Bill. To my surprise, he was warm and friendly — without the antics. My haircut turned out just fine; even Mom was pleased.

I returned from college to have Ed cut my hair. It wasn't until I joined the Navy that I found there's not much secret to giving a guy a haircut. On board ship, I'd jump into any chair available and let sailors have at me with their clippers. Navy regulations required short and well trimmed hair so it happened often.

That's how I remember it.

LEARNING A LESSON

I knew I shouldn't do it. I had been taught about the evils of stealing and lying since early childhood. Mom and Dad lectured whenever they sensed I was stretching the truth. *What ever had gotten into me?* I asked myself.

Mrs. Lily Smith, our milkman's wife, was my first Sunday school teacher. She seemed to work the topic of honesty into her lesson every Sunday. Miss Braet started on the importance of truth-telling on the first day of first grade. Miss Mackey, who later became a nun, let us know, from the get-go, that anything from our mouths other than the truth was unacceptable in her third grade classroom. Miss Mizer kept up the beat, in fifth grade, by harping on the topic of lying, day in and day out. In one way, or another, lying, cheating or stealing, however slight, did become a way of life for some. Certain kids, well-known to their peers, crossed the line frequently — perhaps, just to "get teacher's goat."

In seventh grade, Miss Mortenson, hit us often with a barrage of reasons why lying was unhealthy, unnecessary and unacceptable. By that time, even some of the better-behaved students had formed habits of fabricating to gain advantage, or, to avoid punishment. Miss Mortenson had penalties that were stiff and embarrassing. She did not forget, or forgive, when caught lying, cheating, or swiping something from another. It was good we had her in our lives, although she was disliked by most. Her definition of integrity was clear. She advocated that we try to develop some as part of our character.

In high school, my participation in sports became major. Coach Nicholas was soft-spoken; he won over his players with his constant concern for their well-being, as well as with his fairness in enforcing the rules. Being honest with Coach was expected, without him having to lecture about it. Telling the coach a lie was unheard of on his teams; the players wouldn't allow it.

In 1944, World War II was dragging on into its third year. Worry seemed as though it had an effect on people of all ages. Stories of war were on the radio, in the newspaper and on newsreels at the movie theatre. My friend Jimmy, who was a bit younger than me, joined in playing Army nearly every day. One time, as our leader, I decided we should be outfitted with a first aid kit. After some discussion, we decided to visit Davis and White, on Main Street, in Estelline, South Dakota, where we'd both lived most of our lives. The place supplied our town with food, clothing and all sorts of other household items. We decided to go there to "build" an authentic first aid kit to accompany us on our make-believe battle field, in case of injury.

In spite of the structure and emphasis I'd received on being honest, I inappropriately succumbed to the temptation to steal and to disguise the truth. The busy store clerks, Chuck and Buck, paid no attention to our presence, thinking we were there waiting to carry the family groceries for our Moms. Jointly, we lifted a roll of gauze, a roll of tape, and a pair of scissors and stealthily slipped the merchandise into pants pockets. Although we had some money, we made no effort to pay. We scampered out the door with the boast, "By gosh, we pulled it off without a hitch!" As we headed back to the war front to face another fictitious battle, I sensed a rotten feeling in my gut. The seriousness of the "five-finger-discount" we had just taken from Mr. Davis began to sink in. It was like being hit by a bullet!

A call to lunch pulled us in from our imaginary battle field. I was overcome with guilt while we waited in the kitchen for Mom to fix sandwiches. I wondered if she had received a phone call. She happened to notice, with a quick glance, the items we had taken from the store.

"Look what we just bought for our Army first aid kit," I blurted. She gave a strange look, but made no comment. I began to wonder, *Could Mom be getting suspicious?* It was difficult to think straight as I wondered what to say — what to do. Ed Davis, owner of the store, was a dear family friend. He kidded around a lot and treated me like the son he'd never had. His daughter, Jeannie, was like a sister to my brother and me. We played together often. The Roth and Davis families shared holiday meals and celebrations together. We occasionally spent weekends with them at their cabin at Lake Poinsett. *How could I have done this; what am I going to do?* I couldn't bear the feelings I was having.

Next morning, after a restless night with little sleep, I conjured up the courage to speak with Mom. I was nervous, sad and afraid of what my punishment might be. I had yet to speak with Jimmy about my plan to "tell-all." I thought it best if I avoided him. Our friendship was "on the rocks" from the strain of our misdeed. Mom could tell I was petrified as I stuttered and stammered, while trying to tell the truth and explain. She listened, but my voice was feeble and cracking. I wanted to crawl into my foxhole and disappear.

While struggling to find the right words, I managed to spit out my story. Mom's sad eyes looked down at me as she asked, "So, what do you think is the right thing to do, now?" I had no clue. I felt distraught; she could tell. In a calm voice, she suggested I speak with my friend, and then the two of us should go down to have words with Mr. Davis to explain the error in our way. It would be up to him to decide our fate, although she avoided use of that term. I couldn't wait to get started with the recovery plan. Mom's idea sounded simple and logical, but I dreaded having to do it.

I first had to locate my friend and, with artful ingratiation, persuade him to join me in seeing Mr. Davis to tell the truth. After some reluctance, an agreement was struck; we headed for Davis and White. It was our first return to the scene of the crime. We searched, but couldn't locate Mr. Davis. When we asked for him, we were told he was out for the day. We slowly trudged out the door with heads drooping. I knew I would be having another sleepless night. The following morning, bright and early, we presented ourselves before Mr. Davis as he stood by the cash register, waiting to assist with our shopping lists. He couldn't understand why we stood before him speechless — both of us totally speechless. Finally, words came and I did the talking. I stammered through our story and offered to pay for the goods.

"That won't be necessary, if you've learned your lesson," he explained, in a kind tone of voice with a bit of a smile on his face.

I had sure learned mine...and that was the end of it. Telling the truth and receiving forgiveness prompted feelings I've never forgotten. Mr. Davis, Mom and Dad apparently understood the agony I felt. They must have agreed that I had suffered enough. I don't think Jimmy's parents ever learned of the incident. We both had learned a good lesson, regardless.

In the fall of 1950, I was grown; it was time to leave Estelline to finish schooling and find a job. My youth had taught me many concepts; most importantly — crime doesn't pay. The childhood experience with shoplifting taught me a lasting and invaluable lesson. As I went off to earn my fortune, I was depending on the integrity I'd learned as a happy kid in Small-town USA, population 600.

Success in my military career depended heavily on honesty — it was never a problem during the many years I served. The incident with the first aid kit, turned learning experience, had major influence on character development as I grew and developed. The ugliness of my guilt feelings lasted long after, I had difficulty forgiving myself.

That's how I remember it.

JIM, REX AND HARLEY

It was a love affair, no question. I was obsessed. How, at such tender age, could I be so in love? The thrills, the beauty, the power to control me; I was helpless. I had tunnel vision every time I walked by her. I had never felt so "hooked!"

She was a baby-blue Harley-Davidson motorcycle, slightly used and a bit dusty, but beautiful none the less. I had wanted to own, or at least ride, such a bike since age thirteen. My love affair with motorcycles began at age twelve when Glen Lee, a neighbor, brought a high-mileage Indian motorcycle into his yard. It didn't run well. Glen and his buddy, Bud Ludwig, who was the huskier of the two, were often out huffing and puffing as they pushed the rustic Indian around the streets, attempting to make the engine run. I was enthralled with their antics, especially when the engine occasionally fired, belching out a cloud of exhaust and sparks. That engine sure could have used a good tune-up; I had no doubt about it.

In a breakthrough, not long after WWII ended, my brother Bill and I received parental approval to purchase the Doodle Bug motor scooter, on display at The Gamble Store, in Estelline, South Dakota. We spent money saved from our Watertown Public Opinion paper route. Bill took the first ride as he was the older; we were 15 and 13-years-old. I went last, but still recall the thrill of its Briggs and Stratton power, as I raced through the streets. I rode around town that day showing off our newest toy. Folks glanced and stared, it was Estelline's first motor scooter. Although I didn't have to peddle the Bug — it was NO motorcycle.

When the time came for Bill's graduation, from high school, and his departure for college, the Doodle Bug was running rough and low on power, from years of wear and tear. With multiple warn parts, it was ready for retirement. The Bug had given freely of itself, logging many hundreds of hours of pleasure and a ton of miles traveled.

Sadly, I retired Doodle Bug with a heavy heart as it had given so many joyous rides. Soon after, I fleeted up to a Cushman motor scooter after responding to an ad in the newspaper. I now had a royal chariot compared to the Bug, with more power, speed and comfort. There was no sharing required, as the Cushman was mine alone, every day. Soon, I too was off to college and the scooter became my transport to classes, to my off-campus job and for dating.

Then it happened. I was home from college on spring break and walking down to the theatre to visit Dad in his office. Something light blue and beautiful caught my eye as it sat out front a farm implement business on Main Street. Rex, my trusty dog, and I changed direction, and walked straight for the "Harley bike." *I thought, Wonder who the owner of this dreamy speed machine could be. Could it be out front because it's for sale?* We walked on, after spending some time looking it over from wheel to wheel, top to bottom. From that point on, I couldn't get Harley off my mind.

Another day, as I stopped to admire Harley, the implement dealer, Mr. Larimore, saw us standing out front. I was drooling over myself as I was again sizing up the bike, with stars in my eyes. Rex stood by wagging his stubby tail, seeming to realize that I had fallen in love. I must have appeared to be mounted in concrete as I stood motionless, filled with admiration. Mr. Larimore eventually stepped out the door and sauntered over to join the three of us, Jim, Rex and Harley. Then the conversation began.

"It's a beauty, don't you think?"

I had to agree, *"Sure is, where'd it come from?"*

"I took it in trade for a piece of farm machinery, just the other day."

"Mind if I climb on for a minute?"

"No. Go ahead, jump right on, see how it feels." I did so.

"Wow, it fits me just great."

"Do you know how to ride a cycle?"

Then I told a little white lie, *"Sure do."*

"Okay then, do you wanna take her for a spin?"

"Honestly? Are you sure it's okay?" I asked hesitantly.

"Give her a ride...but you'd better stop for gas, she's low on fuel. Got some money?"

"Yup, sure do. Thanks!"

That was all the encouragement I needed. I fiddled with things for awhile until I figured out how to start up. I turned the switch, gave it some choke, set the throttle and gave a kick. The kick-starter was knew to me, but I acted casual, as if I'd "kicked a bike" before. After some fumbling, the engine shuttered and let out a roar. I carefully tapped Harley's shifter into gear and eased out the clutch. Jerking forward, I staggered the bike out onto the roadway. Rex ran along following after Harley, perhaps wonder-

36

*Jim, Rex and Harley, are ready to launch from the
driveway of The Roth House, Estelline, South Dakota, 1952.*

ing if his master had gone crazy. I could hardly contain my excitement. I wobbled down the street, while trying to keep up with things that were happening. I almost struck a small, well-dressed lady waiting in the crosswalk with her shopping bag. She was paying attention, fortunately, and dodged clear just in time.

I gained the knack and felt more comfortable as I motored about town. Rex chugged along behind on foot with his tongue hanging out. The initial ride lead to others as Mr. Larimore seemed to like having me buzzing around town on his "for sale" Harley-Davidson. I tried my best to swing the deal, but my parents said, *"No dice!"* They wouldn't hear of it.

I continued frequent free rides on Harley, thanks to my show of interest and Mr. Larimore's generosity. My parents didn't seem to realize how close Harley and I had become. I gained confidence and a better technique, as I built up seat time. The down side of riding was teaching Rex to climb on with me, so he didn't get left behind. He was a wise old dog that picked up the knack quickly, however his riding along was speed-limited. If I increased speed abruptly, or the ride got bumpy, Rex set himself to leap for safety. I had to be gentle with my driving when he was onboard.

Harley's throttle control worked with a twist of the wrist on the handle bar grip. It was opposite from the throttle control on my scooters. Occasionally, in tight situations, I would increase throttle when *I meant to cut it back.* I had a few close-calls, while in transition. Still, I loved to ride Harley.

The rigors of riding on rough gravel roads were a drawback. Gravel was all we had in and around Estelline except for the asphalt on Main Street. Constant vibration, due to Harley's poor suspension, made my butt and legs grow numb. On longer rides in the countryside, it was smart to stop, park the bike and walk around a bit to get some feeling back. Dust from loose gravel was also a bit of a problem if cars passed, rolling clouds of dust and dirt while tossing small stones at my face. Riding Harley was exciting, but it wasn't always pleasurable.

Eventually, Rex and I decided we must part with Harley. Buying was out of the question. My parent's decision ruled on the issue. I had some feelings of guilt, from using Mr. Larimore's motorcycle so frequently, although he never seemed to mind. Dusty graveled roads, vibration numbness, throttling miscues and the nagging disappointment of my parent's disapproval, worked to terminate my love affair. I had to walk away from the Harley I had used, but never "married." It was a painful breakup for me, but I sensed Rex was a bit happier without Harley on the scene.

That's how I remember it.

RAT TROUBLES

One of the things a mother dreaded most was to have to caution her young children about avoiding the rats in the neighborhood. In Estelline, South Dakota, the late 1930's found such rodents trying to rule, not just in town, but on farms, as well as in neighboring communities. Children were told to run the other direction if confronted by the ugly creatures. Rats were prolific, bold and unpleasant — especially the larger ones. They weren't selective, when they were in your area, they were everywhere.

"We have rats," was unpleasant to say, but admitting as much was the first step in resolving the problem. Efforts by county and city government made rat poison readily available to residents at a relatively inexpensive price — 25 cents per two-quart package. The City Auditor, A.J. Lundberg, made packages of rat poison available, at the bank, where he was employed. People came and the rats began to go — away.

Having hungry outdoor cats and Rat-Terrier dogs helped as they killed and warded off the nasty rodents, but denying rats their habitat was also necessary. Access holes around building foundations and under wooden flooring had to be plugged, or sealed off with metal, or cement. Rats had sharp teeth for gnawing and biting through wood, rubber and other building materials. Humans were cautioned to avoid contact as some rats were rabid and vicious.

Farms had more serious problems, with rats, due to the number of out buildings and the abundant availability of food. Rats favored a menu of grain, spilled silage fodder, dead animal carcasses and food scraps. They hid in dirt piles, weed patches and under the protective cover of lumber piles and old farm machinery.

The little beasts were nocturnal, doing the majority of their feeding, searching and traveling, during periods of darkness. Packs of 50, or more, rats moving and working together were not uncommon. When the food supply wore thin, or when farmers' hostility level grew objectionable, rats would find new areas to invade. Wild rat packs could scavenge and hunt better than packs of hound dogs.

Young farm lads enjoyed the sport of chasing rats and stabbing them with pitchfork tongs. Flooding rats from their holes with buckets of water made for bountiful hunting, but the troops in the bucket brigade had to stay alert in case rats, sometimes as big as cats, struck back with their teeth and claws.

A roly-poly gent named Mr. "Fats" Carlson was a band leader with a converted school bus painted up decoratively, for all to see, as a promotional scheme for his dance band. He and his fellow musicians lived in the vehicle when en route to and from gigs. The bus also served as his personal transportation, it was with him wherever he went. Fats, a well-liked gent, known to many folks in the area, figured out a way to help with the rat crisis. He knew times were tough and money was tight so he "entrepreneured" a discount rat poison sales business to keep busy and to bring in a bit more revenue when the dance band business was slow.

Fats plastered signs, *"Rat Poison for Sale Here,"* on the outside of his bus and peddled the product aggressively, both wholesale and retail. In his spare time, Fats was an avid fisherman, always caring poles and tackle onboard his colorful and overloaded "orchestra-bus" — his pet name for his vehicle.

One cold, foggy winter night, Fats decided to venture out onto Lake Poinsett, said to be South Dakota's biggest natural lake, to try his luck at ice fishing. His lack of familiarity with driving on ice and the reduced visibility in fog proved fatal. A patch of thin ice suddenly appeared in his path with no time to stop the heavy vehicle. Tragically, Fats, his beloved wheels and many, many cases of rat poison sank into a watery grave miles from the shoreline.

It was days before the band leader's fate became known to authorities. When the shocking "Fats news" spread, it saddened his many friends and fans. Dancers in the area sorely missed the showmanship and music of his dance music, but the rats were happy the poison hit bottom. No one ever knew if Fats was drowned, or if he died of rat-poisoning.

With tenacious management of food sources, improved construction, higher levels of awareness, and judicious use of poison, the rat population began to dwindle noticeably. If one farmer was more aggressive in ridding his property of rats than a neighbor, the pack (numbering in the hundreds) would scamper across open farm fields to a new, more lucrative feeding ground. South Dakota farm folks, taking note of rat habits and instincts, worked together to reduce the trouble with rats on their properties.

Cleanliness, assertiveness and cooperative efforts took control away from the rat packs and peace of mind returned to "our neck of the woods."

It was a victory of sorts. However, in the early 1940s, the country found a larger challenge and more serious trouble with new enemies. The Axis "rats" caused us to declare war.

That's how I remember it.

Bill (sitting) and Jim Roth in early spring, at the Sonnenburg House, with Beekman's barn on the right and Beck's house showing just past the barn on the right, it was 1938.

It was a very sad day at The Roth House, shortly after the death of Major Bill Roth, USAF, of cancer. Gram Cathryn and Grampa Les Roth find comfort in Bill's three sons, (L to R) James Scott, Leslie William and Robert Carson, on Easter Sunday 1967.

SLIDING TROMBONE

Whatever in the world got into me? It may have been the slide, the sweet melodic tone, or perhaps it was hope of becoming a successful musician some day. Whatever the case may be, Mrs. Bertha Schou, Estelline High School band director, conned my parents into buying me a used trombone with the promise that she would teach me music and how to play. I was a freshman; easily persuaded into trying new things...that had to be it!

From day one, I had serious doubts...sort of like the day I took my first training flight in a Navy SNJ aircraft. In both incidents, I well recall thinking, *Who am I trying to fool here?* In both situations, I dreaded every moment of instruction; it seemed like wasted time. Mrs. Schou failed to qualify me as a trombonist; the Navy, however, did manage to qualify me as a naval aviator with Wings of Gold — but it took much longer than the norm.

This is about the trombone experience and I kid you not, it was a dreadful one. I quickly learned to play "by ear," but I could not...and never have... learned how to READ music. To help me along, we used numbers written over the notes on the sheet music. Reading notes was just not in my repertoire. My trombone had seven slide positions used to produce appropriate sounds. Being unable to decipher the written musical notes, in order to position the slide to produce the desired tones, made me some sort of a freaky musician, I thought. I knew this and so did Mrs. Schou, but no one else seemed to be the wiser.

Mrs. Schou dragged me out of classes for private lessons in the music room and she dutifully marked up all of my music, with numbers, so I could sit with the band and slide my trombone. Feeling somewhat like a fraud, I went along so as not to disappoint her. She joined me on piano for my trombone solo performances and she insisted I jump up on stage, sweaty and in full basketball garb, to join the pep band while it played to entertain the sports fans at halftime. The trombone episode, in my life, was a weird one, but I did it rather than hurt Mrs. Schou's feelings. When I was lost, or out of touch with the timing of the musical piece, I would continue moving the slide to various positions without blowing even an ounce

Mrs. Schou's Estelline High School Band, in 1949, is made up of the following (left to right): Marilyn Johnson, Garnet Ball, Jeanne Davis, Janet Beck, Yvonne Lundberg, Beverly Archer, Vera Musolf, Lorna Saathoff, Marilyn Ball, Wanda Johnson, Jim Roth, Larry Lee, Ronald Oines, Janet McAtee, Mark Bierscheid. They were the Pride of the EHS Redmen.

of air through the horn's mouthpiece. She went so far as to present me with a miniature trombone pin to display on the BIG "E" on my Redmen athletic letter sweater along with the basketball, football and winged-foot track emblems. It was meant as a reward for my effort, or to motivate me, I guess. Since I was usually the lone trombonist in the band there was no one near me, playing the same instrument, who could figure out just what was going on. I carefully guarded my sheet music so no one would observe the handwritten numbers jotted above each musical note on my "crib" sheet.

I was saved, after two years in the band, when Mr. Blatchford came along to relieve Mrs. Schou as EHS band director. My long black trombone case, with the shiny horn inside, was quickly retired and soon after was returned to the music store for credit. Mom was disappointed as she was a musician at heart and had high hopes that I would someday inherit her ability to play a musical instrument well. To this day, I marvel at every trombone player I hear blasting away with a slip and a slide, producing music that's to die for. I know I missed the boat!

That's how I remember it.

DAD'S PARLOR

The sign out front on the corner of Main, in Estelline, read "ROTH BROS. RECREATION PARLOR," but the folks around town called the place — "The Pool Hall." Dad was 23-years-old when he and his older brother, Milton, came to town, bought the place and hung up their sign. Milton, the silent partner, soon sold his share to his younger brother, Les. Dad was the dynamics of the place, and quickly established a crowd of customers. Working hours were long and hard, as he ran a "tight ship." He was a dedicated entrepreneur.

The building was not in good condition; fortunately, he was only renting. After establishing himself in town, Dad purchased a building in better condition and moved six doors north; next to the bank. The atmosphere didn't change; draft beer was fresh on tap, peanuts in the shell were warm, and times spent on board were good. Three pool tables in the back room were maintained in top condition, with unblemished cloth covers and cushions with bounce. Pool cue-sticks were straight with fresh tips; the chalk and powder were plentiful. Games were on and off during the day, but on Wednesday and Saturday evenings the place was jammed and play went late into the night. Players had to wait in turn to get a game of pool.

I was a young Roth in 1934 when it all began, only two-years-old, but I grew into the business. By age six, I could rack the balls, play a pretty good game, tap an excellent draft beer and roll horse-dice for the house. I knew how to do all of those kinds of things. However, I didn't get to hang-out at the pool hall. Dad broke me in slowly. My usual assignment, when I arrived a bit early to walk home for supper with Dad, was sweeping the place, with a wide and heavy push-broom, using oil-based sawdust compound to hold down the dust. Through the course of a busy day, the customer traffic floor discarded peanut shells, dirt, mud and traces of manure from the farm. Patrons scraped their boots off, on the shiny brass foot-rail at the bar, while guzzling beers, driving away their thirst, spinning yarns and "spreading some bull." Pool hall times were among the most hospitable in town; there was never a shortage of conversation.

Patrons could stand, or sit on stools at the long, highly polished mahogany bar. A couple of booths were placed along the back wall for those

*Estelline's new Roth Brothers Recreation Parlor with
Proprietor Les Roth (center) ready to serve, on Main Street in 1935.*

who wished to take weight off their feet. When gentlemen brought ladies to Dad's parlor they'd usually chose to sit in a booth. Pool, played in the back room, was observed from high-backed chairs, giving spectators a good view of the games in play. Strings of wooden disc-markers hung overhead, on wire lines strung near the tables, for score keeping. Players used cue-sticks to adjust the disc-markers for score. There were two regulation pool tables for playing games of "crazy-eight," or "rotation." A third table, with smaller pockets and under-sized pool balls, was used by the "pool sharks" — usually playing the game of "Snooker" for money. A pair of lamps with green shades hung over each table to illuminate play. It would get rowdy in the parlor sometimes when tall beers and competitive juices energized both the crowd and the pool playing competitors.

Dad's parlor had a little of everything available for serving his patrons' needs. Candy, enclosed in a large glass showcase, sat inside the front door with an assortment of candies, chewing gum, gift boxes, gum drops, lemon drops, tootsie rolls and other sweets. Snicker, Baby Ruth, Mound, But-terfinger, Mars, Hershey bars, plain or with almonds, were popular candy choices in ample supply. Displayed attractively, candy waited on shelves to sooth customers' sweet-tooth cravings. Licorice sticks, salted peanuts, chips and mints added to the variety of goodies for sale. A large strip of celluloid served to protect the contents of the showcase from melting, on days blazing sunlight pierced through the parlor's front windows.

Stacked high on shelves, behind the bar, were tobacco goods of all sorts. Cigarettes by the carton, or pack, a variety of cigars, smoking tobacco, chewing tobacco, snuff, pipes, cigarette holders, pipe filters, even *Prince-Albert-in-the-Can*, were available, in sight, but out of reach of patrons. Free books of matches came with each purchase. For folks who rolled their own, packages of cigarette papers and bags of bulk tobacco were for sale. Pocket-size "roll-your-own" devices were available for purchase, by those not adept at twirling their own stogies, and wishing to avoid the price of "store-bought" smokes. Brass floor spittoons, placed conveniently about, caught the mess from those who chose to chew — if their "spit" was on target. The "Parlor" was Estelline's headquarters for smoking goods; its atmosphere turned blue from hanging clouds of tobacco smoke on busy Saturday nights.

On the side wall, near the booths, were pinball machines for play — at five steel balls for a nickel. Players with the highest scores were rewarded with free games. When players became too ferocious, with the tipping and thumping of the machine, the "tilt light" would illuminate and it was — Game Over! Occasionally, card players took over the lounging booths on rainy days when there was little else to do; their games would often go on until closing.

The days leading up to 4th of July were busy and exciting. The recreation parlor became Estelline's fireworks headquarters. Out went the candy from the large showcase up front and in came fireworks for sale, but safely out-of-reach of children. There were additional fireworks displayed back behind the counter. Dad kept the really big stuff out-of-sight of underage kids. It was a frenetic business as customers came, from far and near, to purchase and create their planned patriotic excitement. For under $25.00, Dad could put together a spectacular family fireworks display. Many had him do so. The long wait until darkness began when the bombs, rockets and roman candles would lit-up the South Dakota sky. There were no fireworks regulations; common sense was the rule.

Dad stocked many miscellaneous items for sale, mostly for entertainment. Punch boards were popular with some who liked to gamble. Top prize money was substantial and you paid per punch, hoping to find the hidden winners. Boards came in varied price ranges — from a nickel to a dollar a chance. Packs of condoms were available, under cover, and sold to those whose needs were so inclined. Those going without were risk-takers; some later found themselves participating in "shot-gun wedding" ceremonies because of their careless ways.

Dad had a knack for knowing things people enjoyed for recreation, and he determinedly tried to serve their needs. During fall harvest time he thought about the farmers, who were his main clientele. He drove to the areas where thrashing crews were working to show them his appreciation of their patronage all year long. With a complimentary keg of beer, packed on ice in the trunk of his coupe, he'd head into the fields. A "free beer break" was an appreciated gesture as was the brief respite from heat and the tedious labor of the day. The limit was one mug per person, so as not to disrupt work in progress. An ice cold beer on a hot, sweaty workday was a welcomed change of pace — while it lasted. Farmers remembered the gesture the next time they came to town and, more than likely, would drop into to Dad's parlor for a couple more — or so.

That's how I remember it.

COAL HEAT

*"Do it now...and **do it right!**"* Dad reminded me. It was my job. He would not let me forget. He chose me as the family member responsible for keeping the coal-fired furnace stoked and functioning well. I was expected to be ever mindful of weather changes and room temperature at our house. A large conventional furnace and coal storage room took up lots of space in the cellar, accompanied by coal dust, ashes, and fire tools of the trade. I routinely, I made regular trips up and down cellar stairs for fire duty. Paying attention to detail was necessary during periods of severe South Dakota cold. I was age eleven and felt equal to the challenge. Dad was my backup, but I dared not falter.

Bulky, dirty chunks of coal were burned in most homes to provide heat. Coal was the fuel of choice in the 1930s and 1940s. Anthracite grade coal was delivered in bulk, to Estelline, by rail in large coal-cars. Purchased by the ton, it was then delivered to home owners by truck. It was the most expensive grade, but it burned hot with the least amount of ash. Lignite coal was burned in the large public school building in town, because it was less expensive, but it was more bulky and the "dirtiest" coal to burn.

When Mom would call out, *"It feels cold in here,"* it was the signal to head for the cellar to perform "fireman duties." Our furnace ate up coal like a hungry dog gobbles its food. Someone had to be responsible for shoveling coal into the fire box on a regular schedule, or flames would burn too low, smolder and die out. It was a sin to let the fire go out and an uncomfortably long wait for adequate heat to return once it was re-fired. When the furnace did go "cold iron," kindling anew was a tedious job, a situation one surely wanted to avoid. The Roth family frequently cut visits and other family activities short in order to be back home in time to salvage a low and dying fire in the furnace.

Eventually, and in the nick of time for me, technology developed a furnace concept called a "stoker." When installed, loaded and set right, the device supplied coal into the firebox throughout the night, while family members and pets slept in the warmth of their beds. Ensuring the stoker had been topped off with coal before retiring was a must-do job, in order to avoid a very cold atmosphere in the house come morning, and I don't mean just the temperature.

Owning a stoker sounded fancy, but its operation remained steps away from automatically controlled heat. We called it "semi-automatic." I was pleased with the device as it meant fewer trips to the cellar for me to check the status of the fire in the furnace. I dreaded nights I'd forget my fire chores before climbing into to bed. Upon remembering, I'd jump out from under my covers and run for the cellar to shovel coal. "Stoking" was a dirty, dusty job but someone had to do it, and that someone was me.

There were other work aspects associated with heating by coal, in addition to shoveling. Ensuring we had an adequate fuel supply meant ordering and paying for delivery, shoveling snow to clear the way for the delivery truck, and hosing down (wetting) coal before it slid down the chute to its cellar storage area. If the job was done with care, it helped reduce coal dust from drifting throughout the house. Shoveling coal kept me busy for months and months. I had expertise in coal-management before most kids my age. I learned early on that becoming a coal miner would not be the career for me.

Coal fires produced ash buildup, in the firebox, that had to be removed on a regular schedule. After being placed in buckets, lugging up the steps and out to the ash pile came next. Over time, fire ash formed into clumps inside the firebox, called "clickers" that had to be broken up and removed manually. I wasn't paid an extra allowance for clinker clearing, it came with the job. A few curse words helped with the big ones that were sometimes almost too tough to break up. Winter seemed to last for an eternity. At times, I wondered if the snowstorms would ever stop their torment. When the warmth of spring filled the house, signaling it was time to let the last fire die, I was ecstatic!

The end of World War II signaled a breakthrough. Everyone was overjoyed and things began to change for the better. V-J Day came in August and before winter arrived we purchased a new home with a bigger and better furnace for me to tend. We upgraded our heating system to propane gas with thermostatically controlled heat a couple of years after the war ended. The furnace pilot light burned continuously and ignited the main burner whenever the thermostat called for heat.

A large propane tank, looking much like a submarine, was buried in the back yard. Refilling was easy, hauling out ashes ceased and there was no more shoveling, coal dust, or clickers. Warmth was guaranteed with little effort. Once the new system was installed, setting the thermostat dial to the desired temperature was all it took to keep warm. It seems so simple after growing up with the awful mess coal made.

I was a free young man with no more shoveling and no more catching hell when the coal fire died, because I had goofed. Ceremoniously, we discarded the coal shovel by sticking it in the garden as 'Mr. Scarecrow' with painted face, twig arms and straw hair. But, wouldn't you know, Dad came up with new chores to keep me busy and out of trouble.

That's how I remember it.

The Estelline Speedway has a crowd on race day, as viewed from the grandstand bleachers, as racers line up for start, in early 1950s.

ESTELLINE SPEEDWAY

"The bleachers collapsed — lots of people hurt!" He exclaimed.

"What are you saying...where?" I asked.

"At the speedway during the variety show...it just collapsed...there's mass panic down there!" Gasping for breath, he stared at me.

I was home from college, managing the movie theatre for my parents so they could take some needed time off. As I stood in the lobby, others came in to fill in the story. The entertainers, a trick horse act, western music singers and a variety of other performers, had the audience worked into some lather. There was hooting, hollering, clapping hands and stomping feet. Suddenly the bleachers began to sway, back and forth — then CRACK! The over-filled bleachers collapsed, plunging hundreds of spectators to the ground in a heap of confusion. The relatively new bleacher construction had yet to pass the endurance test this 4th of July crowd had created. Timber and nails just couldn't handle the exuberance of the celebrants as they let off steam while enjoying the show.

One spectator had a bone in her foot fractured; another had a bad laceration from a long spike nail and was hospitalized. Several were treated for shock; it was miraculous that fatalities were avoided. The entertainers seemed to freeze in place while watching the terrifying scene before them — they had noted the bleachers beginning to sway just seconds before timber and people came crashing to the ground with a crack, crumble and thump. Some spectators scampered to safety while others searched through the splintered and broken bleachers mixed with piles of terrified people. Parents tended to their loved ones and rendered assistance to others who were injured, frightened and hurting. Families were in panic trying to get reunited. Only a few entered the hospital for stitches and casts - some were treated for shock. Janice Davis, Freda Janssen and Mildred Runge were among the more seriously injured. A "dark cloud" seemed to form over the new racing facility thereafter.

* * * * *

In the mid-1940s, after World War II had finally ended, people began to think about new things to do for entertainment and ways to spend

53

It was a dirty, dusty job, but someone had to do it.
Fans looked forward to a bath or shower after a race-day at Estelline Speedway.

On the dirt racetrack with racer #'Lucky 13,' stirring up some dust with
Estelline's towering grain elevators as a backdrop; it's race day!

their leisure time and money. Carl Klein, the Kaiser-Frazier dealer, owned a tract of land south of his dealership. Carl and several other Estelline entrepreneurs decided to construct a new and attractive car race track — they named it, "The Estelline Speedway." Car racing was a bit slow to catch the local people's interest, but eventually regular shows were happening. Local racing enthusiasts built race cars and 'hotshot' racers from neighboring towns, and from other states, came to test their skills. Marv Dewall was an Estelline favorite; he drove hard and loved a tight race. It's been said, "If Marv couldn't beat you, he'd figure a way to dump you!" A "bandit driver" from Woonsocket, South Dakota, came with a fast car powered by a "hopped-up" Model T Ford motor. Wally Warner drove a scary fast '39 Mercury Coupe V-8. The other drivers had to watch out for Wally!

On days of competition, race fan parking was a mess as people filled the track's parking area early and quickly. Overflow parking lined up alongside the passing graveled highway, or parked most anywhere the family sedan could be squeezed in. Local business places near the track had no space for their customers to park. Residents' private driveways were blocked. It grew to be a big problem with no solution. The speedway employees and officials were mostly volunteers. Local band director, Ted Trautman, was the public address announcer and color commentator. His son, Larry, ran the popcorn concession and Ted's wife, Helia, was a racing fan who never missed a race. Watching this new sport in town became a family affair whenever the track was running. Some citizens loved the racing while others wanted it banned.

Speeding racer cars caused several problems. There was noise, lots of it; the threat of injury from crashes; and flying dirt riled up by packs of racers stirring up things. On windy days — hardly ever is there a day in South Dakota without *some wind* — clouds of dirt and dust rose up and drifted aloft to places it wasn't appreciated. Carried by the prevailing southerly winds of summer, the filth traveled north over town, settling an unwanted layer on top of everything. Clotheslines filled with freshly washed laundry, car tops, window sills, window glass, all covered with layers of dust rapidly became the curse of the track. Dense clouds of flying black dirt often obscured race fans' view of cars charging for the checkered flag. The flying dirt problems were aggravated when the track's old watering truck broke down or fell behind. Wetting the track was ongoing between races. The delay gave race fans some time to visit the concession stand and to chat with other fans there to enjoy the newest sport in town.

The unanticipated high costs of track maintenance and administration — staff and officials, trophies, purse money, grading, watering, insurance, publicity, risk of rainouts and dwindling crowds — began to strain the logic of continuing to run the track. Recollections of the 4th of July bleacher collapse turned some fans away, never to return. People questioned the safety of the spectator bleachers at the track. The collapse of the grandstand, years earlier, seemed to spell the fate of the newly developing race track enterprise. It seemed to be the beginning of the end. Almost as quickly as it began, the track's demise became readily apparent to those who were watching the story unfold — and then fold up — forever. Some residents were saddened by the fate of The Estelline Speedway; others were happy to see it die. Eventually, the facility was converted back to farm land. The dirt track was hauled away by the truckload, thus putting an abrupt end to the illegal racing kids and others had been doing on the abandoned property after Mr. Klein closed down the raceway. Trees grew up where race cars once ran and that was the end of that!

My timing was bad; I was away at college during the short life span of the speedway. Otherwise, you can be certain I would have been on that track driving my guts out with dirt flying in my face, having the time of my life. Sadly, it was another of those things I was never able to do!

That's how I remember it.

BLOODY ADVENTURES

What were we to do? We had yet to add "I'm bored" to our rather limited vocabularies. It was before television, VCR, video games, tapes, cell phones, CDs and other "electronic age" devices had come to life. We Roth brothers and our playmates were standard kids of the day, quite creative, capable and intent when it came to joyfully entertaining ourselves. The shortages of the World War II era had an effect on us, but we didn't seem to mind. Toys, even board games, were scarce. Playing cards, Lincoln logs and a cheap erector set were about all we had to fiddle with. Yet to reach our teens, we had a lot to learn.

As luck would have it, we had numerous opportunities to involve ourselves right in our Estelline neighborhood with, or without, parental approval. Our sense of inquisitiveness drove us in all directions; we seemed to easily find entertainment...and sometimes trouble. Amazingly, we kept our agenda of adventures to ourselves. The typically cautious and watchful parents we had were somewhat limited in their knowledge of the strategies we used. Their kids put South Dakota's four delightfully different seasons to good use with the variety of "games' they played.

PART ONE

Daily war news reports, on radio and in the newspapers, permeated the minds of everyone so playing "Commandos and Rangers" seemed quite in keeping with the times. A war-game we devised found kids from the "south side" of town called Rangers pitted against those from the "north side" known as Commandos. An imaginary line through the center of Estelline, South Dakota, population around 600, was the line of battle. Our informal style of warfare had no declaration, rules, or defined limits. Crude hand-made forts, shelters, bridges and other creations built by one side were found and destroyed by the other. Seldom did we confront the enemy; most destruction was done secretly without personal contact. We occasionally carried slingshots with a few small rocks in our pockets for ammunition, but such weapons only came into play one time.

On a quiet Sunday morning things suddenly got aggressive when the Rangers invaded, trying to takeover Commando control of Ludwig's barn,

Brothers, Bill (top) and Jim, show their innocence while contemplating more and better "bloody adventures" about the town.

located just below cemetery hill in northern territory. The battle was a near tragedy. While leaning out an upper deck barn door to observe Ranger positions, a slingshot-fired rock struck my eyeglasses shattering crushed glass into my right eye. Frightened and in pain, I crumpled while war-fighting ended and both sides came to my aid. Brother Bill swiftly escorted my wounded body home for 'parental attention' with his one hand protecting my injured eye and the other toting my shattered eyeglasses.

Mom, upon seeing my bleeding injury, placed an emergency telephone call to Dr. Ed Hoffelt, the local eye specialist, as well as our City Mayor. Fortunately the doctor was at home and after hearing the situation, consented to meeting at his clinic on Main Street to examine my injury without delay. Filled with agony, Mom sat in the darkened treatment room watching the doctor manipulate his instruments as he delicately picked small bits of shattered glass from under my battered and bruised eyelid. It seemed an eternity before the picking ordeal ended. Sent home with ointment oozing from under my newly fitted black eye patch, I was told to rest and to take it easy so healing could occur. A week of guarded care followed by a thorough re-exam revealed my vision had been spared.

"Had he not been wearing his eyeglasses at the time, Jim most likely would have lost vision in that eye — permanently," Dr. Hoffelt declared, as he dismissed me with a clean bill of health and a warning to play more carefully in the future.

In the days that followed, the Commandos and Rangers struck an unspoken truce ending their "war games" once and for all. Peace returned to the streets of Estelline though the world war blazed on and on — changing some blue stars to gold in the windows of our town.

PART TWO

A lonely ramshackle building set on the backside of a hill just north of town appeared to be abandoned. It invited adventure. One day at play our youthful curiosity drove us to investigate the mystery of this place we'd been wondering about. The "hut" was located on a seldom-used dirt road just off the gravel highway not far from the farm house our family was renting on the northwest outskirts of Estelline.

As several of us cautiously approached the rather dilapidated structure, we were greeted by a strong sickening odor. We paused momentarily to debate the advisability of continuing. Curiosity overpowered good judgment as we proceeded. A worn, poorly fitted door hung slightly open on one bent and rusted hinge. Had it not been ajar, perhaps we would have stopped in our tracks, turned and walked away. However, instead we barged headlong into the dark and dinghy space; our sense of adventure invited a closer look. The putrid smell caused us to stop breathing during the seconds it took for our eyes to adjust. Then we froze, realizing what we'd come across. The place was splattered with dried blood as if it had been painted red with a brush. Body parts, hide, bone and hair from animals were strewn about. We thought the place was a messy disaster. Large steel hooks used to hang skinned carcasses dangled from an overhead beam. A very large steel kettle, similar to the type used by witches for brewing was the room's center piece. It was partially filled and most uninviting to investigate.

It became readily apparent to us that this shack was in an out-of-the-way place for good reason. We shuttered, holding back our urge to vomit, as we realized we were standing in a slaughter-house where livestock was brought for "processing." We were all too brave to chuck our guts — we hoped!

Not one of us had ever given thought to how a steer or hog became a steak or pork chop on our dinner plates. Farm animals were brought here to be killed. It was the first stage of cutting meat which we'd often witnessed at butcher shops in Estelline's several grocery stores. Tools used to kill and dismember animals hung from racks covered with slaughter residue. Without delay we spun about easing ourselves out of the place as we ran top speed for the hills. Our discovery was never discussed nor did we return again for another look. We agreed we'd never tell our parents of our discovery. Later, whenever I saw a package of meat from our butcher or a serving of meat on my dinner plate, I had ugly flashbacks!

PART THREE

The smoldering, odiferous collection of abandoned stuff in a previously over-mined gravel pit was a place known in Estelline as the town dump. The dump had no fence, gate, supervision, or regulations. It wasn't meant as a place to come for entertainment, but it was a spot where youngsters, as well as adults, congregated to enjoy snooping, as well as to amuse themselves with the things they'd find. It was in the late 1930s and early 1940s, a period when anyone could come anytime to get rid of most anything — and they did!

Located on the highest hill in town, at the north end of Main Street, the dump was coincidentally adjacent to the Hillcrest Cemetery, called the graveyard by kids. In later years, no doubt by popular demand, the dump was moved to a more appropriate location. Trash pickup was optional in town and arranged for privately at your own expense. Most citizens carried their own garbage and trash to the dump, or burned it in used 55-gallon oil barrels located in the alley behind their property. The dump was a busy and popular place. You just never knew who you might meet while there.

Accumulations of trash were often set ablaze to reduce the bulk. Burning junk smoldered for days at a time until heavy rains came along to douse the flames. Smoke and putrid odors often turned away the faint of heart that occasionally came, out of curiosity, to find treasure. The place was unpleasant upon arrival, but after a time it became no bother. Clouds of smelly smoke belched and drifted about with the wind. This huge man-made hole in the ground seemed a logical place to haul and dump unwanted things. Stuff had to go somewhere and this pit was it. Rats, near the size of cats, thrived on an abundant supply of spoiled and decomposing food delivered to them regularly. Gravel trucks that hauled material to spread on county and state highways were replaced by trash trucks bringing in building debris, junk, garbage and waste.

The pit we called the dump was a sorry sight of worn and useless items; appliances, auto bodies, tires, machinery, paint cans, motor oil, dead animals, broken toys, clothing, aged furniture — the place was a paradise for scroungers. It was a most interesting place where one person's trash became another person's treasure. Adults frequented the dump to search for reusable and fixable items while kids came there to amuse themselves. Many things of interest waited to be discovered. Searching for treasures was an addiction for some. Some people hauled away more things than they came to dump. Observing scavengers work at their trade and finding things that were "keepers" was entertaining. The rats came out mostly at night which made dump activities low risk. Sports hunters came at night with rifles and spotlights to sharpen their shooting-eye and to help the city hold down the rodent population.

We often supplemented our weekly allowance by searching for recyclables: hunks of bronze, brass, copper, steel and rubber, to exchange at the salvage yard for spending money. Whittemore Hatchery, on Main Street, used the dump to discard chicken eggs that had failed to hatch in the incubators. Occasionally, the blazing sun continued to warm discarded eggs until little chicks popped out to scavenge for food. We'd hurry to the rescue and take them home as pets. The chicks usually survived for the

61

summer, but were harvested for dinner before winter set in. We quickly became oblivious to the odors and ugliness of the dump once our adventurous activities began and they usually did shortly after our arrival. We avoided freshly deposited and still fuming trash piles as we worked our way through the stuff at the dump.

Wintertime was best for play as the heavy snow cover made it more user-friendly. Seldom were fires burning and the layers of snow and ice minimized the dump-smell. Heavy snowfall made for some excitingly steep sled runs down the banks of trash. Sledding trails were short and fast, but there were those obstacles to dodge. Steering the sled was critical and hazardous at times. Participants were severely challenged and adrenalin was pumped...we planned it that way.

While zipping down one of the "expert" runs, lying face-down on my sled, I "zigged" when I should have "zagged," and had to confront a large cook stove at the bottom of the trail. Fortunately, the oven door was removed and as I sailed into the oven and out the back-side, I acquired a rip in my snowsuit and a missing left mitten. Lifting from my sled, I observed a red streak in the snow near me. It was blood — mine! Friends cheered my daring stunt, but shouts ended quickly. A deep slit had been cut in my left wrist when my speedy sled and I struck the rear of the rusty oven while passing through. Blood was spewing heavily enough to give me a fright. Dropping my other mitten, I clamped my right hand tightly over my left wrist and high-tailed it for home. Getting some repairs and a tetanus shot at the hospital were the easy part. Telling Mom a story, different from what actually happened, was the challenge.

The dump was an adventure in a place not fit for kids. We knew it, but who was going to tell a parent and ruin the fun? No one ever did!

That's how I remember it.

FLY WITH ME

Flying was enjoyable and rewarding when the flight crew saw 'eye-to-eye.' Two U.S. Navy Commanders, Bombardier-Navigator Van Westfall and Pilot Jim Roth, were a close-knit team in the era, 1970-1971, at Navy/Grumman Faciltiy on Long Island, New York.

SECRET FLIGHT

The telephone rang. "It's for you," my wife sang out. Bente handed me the phone as I swung around the corner of the garage. Luckily, I took the call on a walk-around phone so I could step outdoors to talk. It was my eighty-some-year-old friend, Bill Sendell, of Lindenhurst, New York, calling from Bayport Aerodrome where he hangared his prize 1946 Piper Cub J-3. Bill's wife had gone out of town. He seemed lonely and was apparently looking for some companionship — perhaps someone to go flying with him.

"Wanna do some flyin', Jim? The weather's great and I'm out here at the hangar."

"Aahh...sure do...I'm on my way. I'll be there in about 30 minutes!"

"Good, I'll meet you at the gate."

"See ya soon, Bill. So long for now."

I pondered for a few seconds about whether or not to tell my wife what was up. I quickly decided to skip the details for now.

"What's that all about?" Bente asked as I came indoors.

"Oh, my friend Bill needs a hand with something, that's all. He's out at his hangar. I'll be home in time for dinner...bye."

I jumped behind the wheel and sped off in my Beamer, holding speed at about ten over. I didn't want to miss my chance. It was already 2:00 p.m. and daylight was only going to last a few hours more. Noting the weather was unusually beautiful, I thought, "What a spring-like day in January." Driving with rooftop open and wind tossing my hair about further tweaked my appetite for some flying.

Bill greeted me with a warm handshake and wide smile; it had been some time since we last spoke. He proudly conducted a detailed tour of his hangar hang-out. The kitchen, sleeping area, head, and loft lounge had all the comforts of home. There were trophies, photographs, models, tools and many airplane parts stowed on racks and shelves throughout. I was impressed with his neatness and organized layout of his keepsakes.

Sitting proudly as the hangar's center piece was the most beautifully restored and highly polished yellow J-3 Piper Cub I'd ever seen. Bill and his son had recently completed a major restoration job on this, his prize possession. For more than two years he'd been promising me, "We'll go flying one day, soon as the Cub is ready."

Bill flicked an electrical switch that set his "jury-rigged" hanger door mechanism to work. Slowly the huge doors growled and rumbled open. Together we carefully coaxed the Cub out onto the grass parking area for startup. Cautiously, we ensured ample wingtip clearance on both port and starboard wings. As we rolled his "baby" out, at a snail's pace, we discussed flight planning. I was to fly up front. He would ride in the rear seat to back me up as I familiarized myself with the flying characteristics of the Cub, an aircraft I'd not flown before.

It was a tight fit. I struggled getting myself wedged into the front seat and my harness straps buckled, even with help from Bill. My large feet, outfitted with a pair of clumsy boondockers, smothered the tiny rudder pedals. Manning the controls, I gave the all clear signal for Bill to kick the prop through for start. With one flip of the propeller, the petite Cub engine fired into idle RPM with a smooth and hushed "putt-putt" sound. Power sufficient to get the Cub airborne awaited its call.

Bill removed wheel chocks, slipped into the rear seat, hooked up safety straps and readiness for taxi was set. Aerodrome course rules and flight planning were discussed as we awaited the engine oil to warm up a bit before we increased power for taxi. Soon we were in motion and S-turning to clear traffic ahead en route to the take-off area of the grass covered aerodrome. Bill stopped the Cub for engine run-up and magneto checks. All was good to go as we rolled into position. I felt the thrill of flight tweaking my senses as the Cub's mighty little engine reached full power. The excitement of defying gravity filled my inner being, once again.

Quickly we began to pick up speed as we thumped and bumped along down the grass strip for liftoff. As the Cub broke ground, Bill turned over control for what was an uneventful climbed to 800 feet altitude and level off. I flew some basic air work over Long Island's Great South Bay: banks, dives, climbs and precision turns. Things were going well so we headed back into the aerodrome landing pattern.

I was calm but damned excited. I hadn't touched flight controls of an aircraft in 31 years! That previous flight had been a Navy production acceptance test flight in an F14 Tomcat from Grumman Calverton airfield on eastern Long Island, in 1975. Speeds to Mach-2 (1250 MPH) at 35,000 feet altitude, pulling 7-Gs were the routine in Tomcat. We topped out in the Cub at 800 feet altitude with flying speed between 80-90 MPH. My long

*Bill Sendell (not pictured) and his Piper J-3 Cub are about
to go flying with Jim at Bayport Aerodrome, Long Island, New York, January 2006.*

unused flying skills came back quickly as if they had been waiting for a call and wondering, "Would I ever be calling upon them again?"

Bill guided us down on the first landing in a right hand approach, according to the aerodrome's landing pattern course rules. During my many years of Navy flying, left hand turns to touchdown were the norm. I felt a bit uneasy, perhaps weird, on my first couple of right hand approaches. Soon I picked up the knack as we continued stop and go landings until dusk. Frankly, as far as I was concerned, it was getting uncomfortably dark!

Bill finally remarked, "Without running lights and a landing light, we're pushing flight rules just a bit." He called our mission complete as we made the final touchdown.

After return to the hangar and engine shutdown we carefully and lovingly placed the Cub back into her cozy hangar cocoon. What a day! What a flight! What fun! After a short drink of his favorite wine, I thanked Bill with a warm handshake and loads of sincerity. I stumbled down the pathway to the parking area in darkness, jumped into my car and headed for home. During the drive, I dialed my cell to announce an impending arrival for dinner.

"Where are you? It's late. It's after dark. We're waiting dinner for you," were Bente's words that smacked me back to reality. I had been gone much longer than expected. My wife had developed some concern, I could tell.

"I'm ten minutes out, pour the wine."

"Don't be funny. Just hurry up!"

"Roger, out."

Now for the secret; how am I going to spring this one on her? I thought. Since my Navy retirement from flying, Bente had caringly discouraged my further participation in flight. She took my news pretty well, but was a bit taken aback while I eased out the story of the flight and how well things had gone. It made for exciting dinner conversation, so I thought.

"Some fun," I commented with a wide grin. "The Cub is so small, you feel like you're wearing it."

"I thought you were finished with flying. Is your life insurance paid up? I hope so!" were Bente's last words on the topic, for the moment.

It was a day of secrets and surprises, but dinner was neither. It was as usual – delicious. Now that the secret was out, it took days for Bente to stop talking with her friends about my being "up in the air." She's cleared me for further flight, the next time Bill calls.

That's how I remember it.

Epilogue:

It's been said that - *"The Piper Cub is the safest airplane in the world; it can just barely kill you."* Max Stanley (Northrop Test Pilot)

TAMING A TEXAN

The Yellow Peril, J-Bird, SNJ, *Texan,* and other pet names it was called, could be a handful of trouble for novice airmen striving to prove they were, "safe for solo." In the 1950's, the North American *Texan* was one of the aircraft used by the Navy and Air Force to train primary flight students longing to earn a set of pilot wings. The dual piloted, single engine, low wing aircraft was demanding and unforgiving; it was one of the very best basic trainer aircraft ever built. The *Texan* could accelerate you heartbeat in seconds if due respect was not rendered during flight. No sissy ever soloed in a *Texan.* Young lads, arriving for flight school at Navy Pensacola's Cradle of Aviation, received a rude awakening the first morning they strapped in. Suddenly the day of donning Navy *Wings of Gold* seemed almost out of reach. It was a handful of airplane.

At the beginning of each training day, rows and rows of idle yellow *Texans* sat on the flight line looking like flocks of seagulls contemplating the wind, the weather and where to find their next meal. Nostrils cringed at the whiff of high-octane aviation fuel, engine oil, hydraulic oil and residual exhaust fumes as you approached. The scent was that of *Texan*. As you entered the cockpit the odor got worse. Over-priming the engine, on start, sent a strong smell of raw fuel up your nose and it meant, "look-out for flames." If you under-primed, puffs of smelly smoke belched from the exhaust stacks as cranking continued uselessly. The smell of engine oil and hydraulic oil, occasionally mixed with vomit, emanated from the cockpit bilge where fluids pooled, but were difficult to reach for removal. Florida sunshine ripened the concoction, as heat fermented the pollutants. By the time engine-start was accomplished your mind was busy monitoring gages, following the plane captain's direction signals and preparing for taxi. Smell was superceded by other priorities.

Student pilots were ever mindful of the instructor pilot sitting in the rear cockpit closely noting performance. A voice on the intercom usually meant you had screwed-up procedure, or directions given during pre-flight briefing. A tail-dragger, the *Texan* required use of alternate wheel braking and left, or right, rudder input while S-turning to ensure clearance ahead while taxiing during ground operations. The large radial engine, cowling

The SNJ-Texan trainer gave Navy student pilots all they could handle.
Jim soloed in it on 14 April 1956 while training at Whiting Field, near Pensacola, Florida

and spinning propeller severely blocked forward visibility. Wide sweeping turns allowed the instructor some forward visibility from the rear cockpit. The instructor was responsible for safety both on the ground and in the air even if he wasn't at the controls. With a raised voice the instructor pilot gave frequent safety cautions and flight instructions, while up front the student was primarily engaged with listening, lookout and headwork.

Receipt of clearance for takeoff, from the control tower, tweaked the student's anxiety level to a new high. Taking a deep breath, along with an enthusiastic gulp, helped place the heart down where it belonged as the throttle was advanced for take-off power. Thoughts of *headwork, concentrate,* and *DO NOT screw up* raced as the ground below grew smaller and smaller. Heading for the practice area, at cruise altitude and airspeed, gave the student pilot a few moments to mentally review instructions received at the pre-flight briefing back in the hangar. Proper safety lookout, correct procedure and demonstrated ability to fly assigned maneuvers were the criteria instructor pilots used for grading. The sky over Pensacola was yellow, with *Texans,* as student pilots conducted flying labs to hone their skills. There were no free rides; flight training was serious business from start to finish. Smiling and joking were saved until the mission was complete. Learning to *fly right* demanded all you could give! Executing turns, climbs, dives, rolls, loops, barrel-rolls, precision touch and go landings, stalls, spins and recoveries, practicing emergency procedures and navigation took up more than an hour per training flight. Instructional flights were stressful and they were meant to be just that. The *Texan* was good at weeding out those who were not suited to be pilots.

Returning to base, entering the landing pattern and executing a safe recovery were no time to let down your guard. A complacent attitude, before *Texan* was safely on deck and in the chocks with engine secured, could be fatal. Body odor added to cockpit smells by flight's end. Instructor pilots left students in silence to wonder during the stroll back to hangar debrief area for critique. Yearning for approval or something positive from the instructor's lips kept the pressure on long after engine shutdown.

The smell remained; only a good hot shower and laundry service could rid pilots and their flight suits of the odoriferousness of the *Texan.* Performance expectations and stress increased as headway through solo, precision, acrobatics, formation, night flight, gunnery, dive bombing, instrument and carrier qualification phases progressed. Successful completion of the basic flight-training syllabus took many months. Advanced training followed for those who made the grade. Taming the *Texan* was the first challenge; some trainees were unsuccessful! They were sent away to look for another profession.

I successfully tamed the *Texan,* in 1956, by safely completing the basic training requirements including six carrier arrested landings on the USS Saipan, a straight-deck aircraft carrier operating in the Gulf of Mexico, off NAS Pensacola. I advanced to jet training phase in Corpus Christi, Texas and receive my Navy Wings of Gold in April 1957. Surprisingly, I was ordered back to Pensacola as a flight instructor in the *Texan.* I logged 1,200 flight hours in the Texan by the time I reported to my sea duty squadron to fly the A4 Skyhawk, in 1958. The *Texan* and I parted as "dear friends." I credit my confidence, flying skills and flight safety record to lessons learned and taught in the *Texan.*

That's how I remember it.

Jim Roth and Van Westfall flew and accepted the final A6A Intuder attack aircraft at Grumman Calverton Facility, New York, on December 16, 1970. The little red lantern painted on tail section signifies the end of the line for the Navy's A6A. The updated A6E model followed in great numbers.

TROUBLED INTRUDER

Piloting a new production A6 Intruder on a Navy acceptance test flight near Grumman Calverton airfield, had been routine to this point. Suddenly we were dealing with an in-flight emergency. My bombardier-navigator (B/N), seated next to me in the cockpit, was puzzled. I was as well. Neither of us had seen anything unusual while completing a hard 360 degree turn at 8,000 feet altitude. As I advanced throttles smartly to full power to regain lost speed, we heard a thud and then strange sounds as an engine flamed out.

Loss of an engine, in flight, is rare, it means instant trouble. I pondered hastily, "How bad are things going to get?" We didn't know. We could only anticipate the worst while hoping for the best, a virtue that serves airmen well. Years of training and flight experience were my preparation, for dealing calmly with airborne difficulties, no matter what the circumstance. During my 20-year flying career, I'd flown 5,500 pilot hours, in an array of Navy aircraft with an occasional minor emergency. I now was experiencing my first mid-air collision with, subsequent engine failure. My 3,000 flight hours in the Intruder qualified me to handle most any airborne emergency, so I hoped.

Here's a call for "the right stuff" — 'twas time for *attention to detail!* Commencing emergency procedures, we glanced about quickly and listened intently. While assessing the situation, we evaluated the logic of attempting a return to Grumman. One engine was out, and there was no telling if the other might fail. We had an aircraft with unknown damage, but it seemed flyable. In time, further problems could be developing, we just didn't know.

As I hit the dump switch, and observed fuel spewing a trail in the sky behind us, I gently turned towards home. Reducing weight made for safer approach speed and landing. As I scanned engine performance indicators continuously, I sized up what more I could be doing to help save the day. We grasped for better understanding of what had apparently struck the Intruder, setting up the anxious scenario that was unfolding.

"Just how hairy is this thing going to get?" I asked my crewmate, knowing that he had no answers either. In short order, we agreed that it was doubtful a collision, with another aircraft, had occurred.

The situation seemed less critical as we continued, with no new problems. With our plate full already, the good engine kept going, we had flying speed, a safe altitude and normal feel on the flight controls. A quick situation overview eased tension, but confidence in how long things would last was shaky. The fact that I was strapped to an armed ejection seat with a parachute and survival raft didn't enter my mind. There was an unspoken shared feeling, in the cockpit, that we'd be able to get back on deck safely. Adrenaline was pumping and our "can do" spirit took over.

Keying the mike on my UHF radio, I called to alert Grumman of our airborne emergency.

"Grumman Tower, this is Grumman - 52, over?" I then gave a brief report of our predicament. Tower confirmed receipt of my message, then requested our position and intentions.

"We're out east, near Orient Point at around 8,000 feet. A collision with something has wiped out the starboard engine. We're declaring an emergency and heading your way...request straight-in approach with priority landing clearance."

"Grumman - 52, please say again, your transmission is breaking up." Gail, the tower operator, barked at us assertively. She sensed trouble.

This gal was one of the best. I repeated my words slowly so she'd grasp and understand the details in order to quickly pass information along to airfield emergency personnel. Launching the helicopter rescue team and alerting flight operations was step one. Gail's questions came in rapid-fire order. As her interrogation continued, I kept my responses orderly and professional. Timely coordination of the emergency effort was her job. Getting the Intruder back on the runway, in one piece, was my job.

Another radio call came:

"Grumman 52, this is Grumman Tower, over?"

"Go ahead, Tower."

"Call, runway in sight."

"It'll be soon, very soon."

"We're rolling crash equipment at this time.'

"Thanks!"

"Request present range and heading inbound."

"15 miles...220 degrees."

"Report present altitude."

"Passing 5,000 feet, descending for 'straight-in' to Runway 22. Gear and flaps coming down. Please check us visually. Is arresting gear rigged? Just in case of brake failure?"

"Roger, we're rigged. Request fuel state. "

"Fuel...1800 pounds."

"Roger, keep tower advised."

"Grumman - 52, will do. Thanks."

While radio chatter was carrying on, in the cockpit, we were busy flying, adjusting and gaining confidence that we'd make it back safely. The smell of jet fuel after the thud and engine flame-out had dissipated. Chance of fire, or the likelihood of jet fuel leaking internally, was slight, so we rationalized. I kept a keen eye out for glowing fire warning lights which meant *eject...eject,* no questions asked! Our confidence grew as things stayed relatively calm, as far as we could tell.

Scurrying through cockpit checks and emergency procedures in an effort to stay ahead of things kept us fully occupied. I worked up a heavy sweat racking my brain to ensure that I didn't omit anything important. My crewmate strived to track and record order of things, as they were happening. In depth mission debriefing sessions routinely followed completion of Navy acceptance flights. This wasn't normal routine. We strived to be well prepared with comprehensive details.

With the dead engine's hydraulic system inoperative and the probability of having further hydraulic system difficulties, I lowered the landing gear and flaps early to ensure wheels and flaps down for touchdown. As the duty runway came into view, so did the reassuring sight of a line of fire and crash trucks on the roll.

Aircraft assembly line workers, metalsmiths, electricians, electronic technicians, engineering specialists, jet mechanics, support systems specialist, troubleshooters and company executives toiled for many thousands of dedicated man-hours building Intruders, Prowlers and Tomcats, all mainstays in our nation's defense posture. The reputation for building only the best carrier-based weapon systems taxpayer money can buy instilled strong employee pride. Navy flying personnel, in appreciation of Grumman Aircraft Corporation's good work, referred to the company affectionately as, *"The Grumman Iron Works."* Safety of flight and excellent performance were the company's traditional workmanship signature.

*The Navy aircrew, Pilot Jim and Bombardier-Navigator Dick Schram,
climb onboard a production A6 Intruder, with the intent of having a
trouble-free acceptance test flight. Hey, you never know.*

Back in the cockpit, we knew from experience, as word spread of an "airborne emergency inbound" wide-eyed observers would scoot for the windows, or out front open hangar doors, to watch. It behooved us to demonstrate professional airmanship as we nurtured a troubled single-engine Intruder to touchdown. The sight of a virgin A6 aircraft, having just experienced spreading its wings, limping home, with its crew struggling to land safely, unquestionably aroused anxiety among those watching.

Working the Intruder towards runway touchdown was going well, almost with ease. Seeing shiny red crash trucks racing down the runway, in our direction, was reassuring. Feeling the "sweet clunk" of runway contact brought stress levels a welcomed relief. Our short rollout was anti-climatic. Once stopped, before engine shutdown, a flight line crewman crawled under the Intruder to insert landing gear safety pins to safeguard against inadvertent collapse. Firefighters in full battle gear crept close with fire foam lines charged as they aimed their shiny hose nozzles at the Intruder, in case fire broke out. Quickly, and with a true sense of appreciation, I shut-down the good engine that had given us sufficient thrust to return safely.

In short order, a waiting tractor hooked to the Intruder for tow to the parking area and post flight inspection. We became the center of attraction, as a mega welcoming committee: mechanics, engineers, flight test big-wigs, Navy personnel and curiosity seekers gathered to view damaged to the Intruder. Learning more details and the truth of the matter followed. Bleeding red hydraulic oil and looking battered, the sturdy aircraft had returned with its crew, avoiding disaster. Hearty pats on the back and firm handshakes brought broad grins as we strolled back to the hangar for debriefing. The pressure was off; the relief felt damn good.

Not until after extensive post-flight inspection did we learn that a goose, or maybe a couple, had been ingested in flight. The engine was destroyed. Goose bones and feathers were found in the intake duct and throughout the engine. Fan blades from the compressor section had broken loose and passed into the hot turbine section where power is produced. Quick stoppage had caused engine implosion hurling steel blades out front of Intruder. A hail of shrapnel pelted the aircraft as it passed through the flying debris.

With hydraulic oil spewed inside and out, from severed oil lines, the aircraft was a bloody mess with bad smells to match. Upon implosion, the engine's flying compressor blades were like small knives, cutting and dent-ing as they hit and penetrated the aircraft. The sturdy Intruder proved durable and capable enough to survive *"the goose's noose."*

Further inspection found the good engine's throttle cable partially severed by flying turbine blades. The few strands remaining intact provided throttle control sufficient to allow completion of the flight to touchdown. We were lucky things turned out as they did. Crew ejection would have been the alternative had the damaged throttle cable parted while in flight, rendering the remaining operable engine useless.

The freaky bird strike incident had several "ifs and buts." It was the first time in my career I'd made contact with a bird in flight. Bente, whom I'd kept in the dark, first got wind of my Intruder being *"goosed"* when she overheard the story, told at a social function, some weeks later. That evening, during our drive home to bed, the question came up.

"What else, do you suppose, is going to happen these last weeks before you retire?" I smiled, winked and kept driving.

That's how I remember it.

Epilogue:

The day my Intruder had its incident with a goose was 34 years ago. The recent TV news story of the US Air flight that was "double-goosed" and forced to ditch in the Hudson River was a wakeup call for me. Bente and I watched the coverage for hours. Her questions and our discussion brought back vivid memories. I jumped on my computer and cranked out this memoir. US Air's Captain "Sully" had a much tougher job to do — he had 155 lives to save.

CATSHOT

Man found a way, early on, to land aircraft on the deck of a ship. Soon it followed that they solved the tricky task of launching aircraft from the flight deck, as well. A challenge came when aircraft became too heavy to deck launch. Some form of "help" was needed in order for heavily loaded aircraft to achieve flying speed. The aircraft carrier's catapulting system, much like an early warrior's slingshot, was born.

Different methods of catapulting were tried, but the system that lasted the longest, and is still in use on present day aircraft carriers, is the steam-powered catapult. The power to overcome inertia is generated from fresh water, converted to steam, by nuclear reactors, or oil fueled boilers. Ample supply of steam and proper maintenance of catapult machinery are factors critical to safe operation. Lack of manufactured fresh water, or the inability to produce sufficient steam, can delay carrier flight operations seriously. Breakdowns, or failure of catapult machinery, can send flight crewmembers to a watery grave. Sailors selected to maintain and operate the carrier's four catapults are carefully screened. "Cat-shot" is the name given to the evolution of launching by catapult. There is no doubt this is one of the most interesting and exciting operations involved with carrier flight operations. Flight crews manning aircraft and flight deck sailors involved with catapulting have great respect for their responsibilities. This is not a routine operation for there are numerous checks and rechecks in the process. Heart rates are accelerated when it comes time to catapult for there is much at stake.

When a catshot fails — it has been known to happen — the aircraft is unable to achieve flying speed. It's called a "cold" cat-shot. Crashing into the sea results and flight crew fatalities are probable. Without question, the aircraft is lost, crew rescue procedures are implemented and do save lives sometimes. Quick action and luck are what determine the fate of the flight crew. Crashed aircraft sink rapidly and the carrier lacks the maneuverability to avoid overrunning the wreckage in the sea, ahead of the ship. Carriers travel 25-30 nautical miles-per-hour during launching of aircraft; it takes several miles for the 90,000-ton vessel to stop, or reverse course. Rescue helicopters and "plane guard" surface ships are routinely stationed,

*Jim, with Attack Squadron - 64 Detachment, awaits hydraulic
"Catshot" from bow of USS Wasp, CVS-18, in North Atlantic, 1962, in an A4 Skyhawk."*

at the ready, to render assistance in case an unfortunate flight crew ends
up in the water.

When launching from the carrier flight deck, sailors in yellow jerseys
direct aircraft as they maneuver to the catapult for hook up. Directors assist
the pilots in their approach to the catapult shuttle. A catapult crew member
affixes the aircraft to the catapult shuttle mechanism by use of a holdback
device made of steel designed for connecting and then to break away the
moment the catapult is fired. The pilot throttles engines to 100-percent
power, "wipes" the control stick to ensure flight controls are free and operating properly, checks engine instruments for normal operation then ver-
bally confirms that crewmembers are ready for launch. All hands position
their bodies erect and firm in the ejection seat. It's the moment of truth, to
"go," or "no go" — the decision is made by the aircraft commander.

When all is set and ready for launch, the pilot renders a hand-salute to
the catapult officer. So doing gives confirmation of the pilot's readiness for
flight and flying speed is the next thing in order. Upon receipt of the pilot's

salute, the catapult officer rotates his arm forward and down to the flight deck. The instant his hand touches the deck, the catapult petty officer, at the control console, touches his finger to the fire-button. Instantly the catapult explodes it load of steam and a 20-ton aircraft fires in motion down the catapult track. There is no turning back at this point...it's a go! The aircraft attached to the catapult's shuttle goes from dead-stopped to 150 miles-per-hour in two seconds! Safe flight is achieved and the sea 80-feet below flight deck level is denied another victim.

Proving you have the right stuff is required before reporting to the carrier for flight operations. The excitement and acceleration by the cat-shot is just the beginning. What follows is a two-hour sortie of aviating through the sky at, or near the speed of sound, often at dangerously low altitude. Each flight ends with a precision approach to the back end of the moving aircraft carrier, for landing. An arrested carrier landing ends the sortie, if you are precise enough to catch a cable (wire) on your approach. The cat-shot and the landing that follows is "what sorts out the men from the boys." It was stated that way *before women became Navy carrier pilots!*

I'm writing to tell you the details of catshot operations onboard a US Navy aircraft carrier because I survived 330 catshots and carrier landings during my career as a naval aviator — and I'm thankful! Would I go there again? Hmmm...perhaps...I'm thinking it over.

That's how I remember it.

Jim Roth and Van Westfall, flight test, inspect and accept a new production Navy A6E Intruder aircraft at Grumman Calverton, New York, 1971.

A close-up shot of Jim Roth in his #605 Skyhawk, 'playing with the clouds during daylight over Norway,' in between his catshot launch and arrested landing on deck of USS Wasp, in 1962 on a North Atlantic cruise.

NIGHT WORK

The hour was late. The night seemed darker than usual. Our heavily loaded A6 Intruder shuttered as we launched off USS Kitty Hawk, on catapult #1. With the powerful jolt from the steam catapult came the reality — *we were airborne and heading into harm's way.* The target area was marginally within range. Top speed, good fuel management, dead-on navigation, and evading enemy threats were challenges lying ahead. Target acquisition, precise weapons delivery and safe return were flight crew goals for the mission. Upping the ante on this assignment was our near zero margin for error.

Brian, my bombardier-navigator, was seasoned with multiple combat missions under his belt. I was a recently reported replacement pilot; sent from CONUS to join carried based Attack Squadron Eighty-Five (VA-85). Brian and I had flown only ten combat sorties together, since my arrival; all had been during daylight. Night operations were a much tougher challenge. My limited combat experience caused some apprehension for both of us. Six squadron flight crewmembers had been lost recently, all at night. Their attrition was part of the reason for me being ordered in from the States. Brian and I shared a common thought - *Do WE have the right stuff?* Time would tell.

Following our catapult launch from the carrier flight deck, the cockpit remained quiet as we skimmed low over the water heading for landfall. Remaining as low as we dared to go to avoid enemy radar detection, we crossed "feet dry" into hostile territory.

"It's a quiet night. This is good. I like it." Brian quipped.

"Is it always like this?" I questioned.

"Hell No! I should say not! It just doesn't figure," Brian responded, with his head buried in the radar hood, as if to be hiding from any hostility that might be lurking.

Chatter then stopped as we busied ourselves with navigation and lookout duties. We were preparing, mentally, for contact with the enemy. Brian worked his radar. I had visual lookout for threats as I monitored aircraft performance and followed computer steering. Fuel management was another concern as I worked the throttles. Air combat survival dictates seeing the opposition before being seen. Onboard electronic sensors warn of hostile threats, but nothing beats the naked eye.

Then, breaking radio silence, I cried out, "Damn, Brian, what the hell is THAT?" Bright flashes shattered the tranquility of the dark night sky. I thought anti-aircraft artillery, or a missile, had exploded near us. Startled and anxious, I craved a quick explanation.

Brian nonchalantly mumbled, "Those are photo flares being fired by recon Crusaders somewhere near us. They're lighting up the sky for some reconnaissance shots for the 'spooks" (combat intelligence personnel).

"Okaaaaay! Nice! But, why weren't we warned? I was about set to eject!" I sputtered, half in fear and half in anger.

"Well, that's just how it is out here at night. We're all doing our best to succeed and survive. Coordination is out of the question, with different units conducting multiple missions simultaneously."

I stared ahead, feeling relieved, but without comment. Time passed as we rumbled along toward the target area.

"Hey, you okay?" Brian asked.

"Yup, no sweat," I replied. But, I could feel my heart rate accelerating as we continued at top speed and deeper into the mission.

Things remained scary quiet, as we barreled through enemy air space. Suddenly, Brian punched my arm, pointing to his radar. He had spotted what we were looking to find. A large enemy truck convoy, carrying supplies, resembled an illuminated snake crawling across Brian's radar screen. The vehicles had doused their headlights, but our high tech detection system had spotted the moving targets in darkness.

"We got 'em, let's hit 'em," Brian's voice was filled with confidence.

"Tally-ho," I shouted, swiping the armament switches to ARMED. I felt satisfaction, finding a significant target, on my first night strike. Flares were fired to illuminate the vehicles and I rolled in, commencing attack.

Grasping the control stick with a death grip, I pressed the bomb pickle, releasing a massive load of ordnance. I yanked back hard commencing a high "G" (force) recovery. Rolling inverted to catch a view, we saw night become day as the wing-mounted multiple-carriage bomb racks dumped their load into the heart of the convoy. Secondary explosions ripped apart trucks loaded with munitions destined for use by enemy forces deep in the jungle below.

"Let's beat it!" suggested Brian, as he switched to computer navigation steering to head us back to *Kitty Hawk*. "Home plate - heading 110

A6E Intruder attack aircraft do their flying very low for protection from the enemy. Night work off the aircraft carrier is its toughest challenge. Jim sharpens his skills with some daytime low level training.

degrees, 275 miles," he directed as he released the face clips on his oxygen mask to wipe away perspiration.

"Damn, there's no time to spare. We've got to hustle to make recovery time. Hang on and keep your hopes up," I replied. The mission was going flawlessly. I felt most appreciative that we had slipped past enemy aircraft, hostile missiles and the always anticipated anti-aircraft barrage of tracers — there had been none of it so far!

Streaking through the sky, we dove for lower altitude heading toward safety. Heading back to sea the darkness thickened. We felt caught up, like flies in a spider web. Higher speed meant higher fuel consumption. Cruising at near seven-miles-per-minute caused us anxiety about our reserve. Calling for in-flight refueling was an option, but working with the airborne tanker, orbiting overhead *Kitty Hawk,* didn't appeal to us as it would delay our recovery considerably. Having eliminated the tanking possibility seemed to perk our confidence. We wanted to keep things simple and not broaden or further complicate our scenario.

I reported, "Intruder, low fuel state," as we closed on *Kitty Hawk,* and began setting up for a straight-in approach. An abbreviated approach was unorthodox for night operations, but we did so to save time and fuel. All hands on deck were alerted and preparing for a "low-fuel landing emergency."

"Got to get her slowed down for a trap (arrested landing), first pass," I emphatically declared to Brian. We had no fuel to spare for a missed approach.

Closing rapidly on *Kitty Hawk,* making its wide wake in the sea below us, well hidden in darkness, we knew she awaited arrival with her ready deck. Landing weight and fuel remaining calculations continued feverishly. Our quick transition from fast cruise to landing speed with no visible horizon was conducive to pilot disorientation. I increased my concentration on scan, and stifled thoughts of how quickly and unmercifully disaster could strike should vertigo, or a miscue, occur.

The hundreds of safe carrier landings I'd accomplished previously did not make this situation any easier. I felt a bit rusty on night landings having just reported to the squadron from shore duty as an emergency replacement pilot. I had no opportunity to "brush up" my carrier landing expertise before reporting to VA-85. My mind contemplated the high tech red-deck lighting on *Kitty Hawk,* which I had yet to experience, causing some extra stress. As we continued to decelerate from fast cruise to approach speed, I worked to assure myself that I was in full control of things. As I lowered landing gear and flaps, I puckered-up my toughness a few notches.

"Intruder, meatball, 1800 pounds," reported Brian to the ship's LSO (landing signal officer) who was there on station to observe, and to assist as necessary, with our attempt to land the Intruder. The orange glow of the meatball on the landing mirror's lens was a beautiful sight — it would mean we were almost home! All of a sudden the night didn't seem so dark.

Flight deck crewmembers were alerted to our position, aircraft type and fuel remaining. Equipment was readied and adjusted for arrestment as our approach continued. We couldn't see the carrier deck and the flight deck crew couldn't see us, but all hands knew a twenty-ton jet bomber was thundering down through darkness of night seeking a safe arrestment on the deck of a ship cutting through the sea at 25 nautical miles-per-hour.

"Roger-Ball," I replied, tightening my hold on the controls, knowing the margin for error was negligible. My job now was to engage the aircraft tail hook with one of the ship's four arresting cables. At this point, Brian was just along for the ride.

"Landing check list complete?" He challenged.

"Roger, complete." I confirmed.

The *meatball* (orange ball of light) we saw was a highly visible image reflected on a concave mirror located on the left side of the landing area. It indicated optimum glide slope for landing. A dim row of white line-up lights on deck centerline gave alignment reference for touchdown. Airspeed was maintained with throttles, controlled with my left hand. *"Check — meatball, line-up, airspeed,"* I repeated to myself, as the landing area on deck rushed toward us.

Final approach was going perfectly until my scan began to breakdown. In close, just seconds to arrestment, the red deck lighting seemed to spook me. I became distracted by taking a quick peek down and forward at the ship's landing area. "Spotting the deck," as it's referred to, spelled trouble. "Meatball, line-up, airspeed," were my "seeing-eye dog" until touchdown. I disregarded my "dog."

It happened in an instant. I lost confidence, concentration and a bit of my "right stuff." Spotting the deck visually, I reduced power and pushed the control stick forward. Landing resulted in a semi-controlled crash! The Intruder slammed down hard, twisting and turning as it stopped abruptly on centerline, *as if by some type of miracle.* The aircraft tail hook managed to snare an arresting cable. The mission was ended — we were spared! Leaning over, I patted Brian apologetically before taxing clear of the arresting gear. I followed the yellow wands of the flight deck directors and taxied forward to park. I ached with professional embarrassment. It had just executed, without a doubt, my worst carrier landing ever!

My confidence appeared to have abandoned me at a crucial point. I broke from standard procedure and dove for the deck. For a flawed second, I couldn't help myself. I doubted our fuel remaining was sufficient to complete a second approach, if we failed on our first attempt to land. My responsibility was to get us on deck. I had used wrong technique in getting us there. The hard landing did no harm to the aircraft, or flight crew, but it gave my pride a hard punch in the gut. A hair-raising, but successful, night combat mission became secondary in my mind as I brooded over my failure to do well on landing. That spastic approach was on the January 25, 1966...it's been stuck in my mind for a long time. It was the last of my 330 carrier landings, although my Navy flying career continued for another ten years. I had to leave the squadron a few days later on emergency leave, back to CONUS. A series of family matters kept me from returning to complete my tour of duty with VA-85 and from returning to carrier flying ever again. Perhaps those stories will be written another time.

That's how I remember it.

Author's Note:

Lieutenant Junior Grade Brian Westin earned the Navy Cross for valor not long after our "night work" together. Brian bravely put himself at great risk while saving the life of his critically wounded Intruder pilot, Lieutenant Commander Bill Westerman. Bill was struck in the upper torso by enemy gunfire while flying at very low altitude on a strike mission in North Viet Nam. Both flight crewmembers were safely rescued after ejecting over water from their damaged Intruder, just off the coast of Viet Nam. Brian was unhurt, but Bill was severely injured. After a long recovery and rehab, he returned to flying Intruders. Brian completed his obligated service and left the Navy.

MOONLESS NIGHT

*Mouth dry...heart rate high...how was it that **I** was scheduled?* My plans had called for catching the late night movie in the pilots' ready room. *Oh well, guess it must be my turn to go out and test the night flying skills,* I thought with a smirk. Making my way on the escalator to the aircraft carrier's flight deck for the midnight launch set my game face. Adrenaline flow began to increase. There was no moon, no horizon, poor visibility. Without visual reference, once launched, from the catapult, cockpit flight instruments would be my "eyes in the night." *Where in the world do you suppose those flight deck control guys hid my airplane this time?* I mumbled as I searched the pitch-black flight deck for a Skyhawk with my number on the side. Movement was an effort, as I trudged about slowly in my bulky rubber anti-exposure suit, flight helmet, steel-toed flight boots, torso-harness, with attached life-vest, survival gear, 38-caliber revolver and band of ammo. I willingly accepted the 30 extra pounds of gear knowing it could be a lifesaver in an emergency.

Navigation bag in one hand and red flashlight with dim narrow beam in the other, it was tough to see through the darkness on deck. The lack of illumination was frustrating and my effort to locate my Skyhawk seemed useless. *How could the catapult fling me into the cold, damp night air if I couldn't locate my bird?* Crazy, but that's what I was thinking. Pangs of apprehension gnawed at my gut. It wouldn't last. Once external pre-flight checks were complete, butt tucked into the ejection seat and strapped, cockpit canopy closed, engine turning, I would be mentally ready. The droning jet engine sound had a soothing affect. It calmed my nerves and instilled confidence. Experience had taught me just that. Exasperation grew as I stumbled along, dodging tools, tie-down chains and flight deck personnel. Other pilots also searched and groped for their "birds." *The first challenge of the night seems to be finding my ride,* I mumbled, with growing impatience. *This is a terribly dark night,* I kept thinking to myself. Stepping carefully, I guarded against an 80 foot free-fall, into the wildly churning sea below. The mammoth rolling swells and wildly frothing waves twisted the carrier into a wallowing snake dance. Carrier pilots are trained to expect nasty flying weather, especially at sea. *This night was shaping up to*

Flight of three A4 Skyhawks in formation are doing a tactics exercise before nightfall. The "moonless" night flight operations from the aircraft carrier, steaming below, await them.

be an ugly one, I declared to myself with a shutter. *Damn, let's get on with the show,* I mused to myself, hoping the mere thought would build my sagging confidence. I bumped my head on my Skyhawk, success at last.

External checks took just seconds, after finding my bird. Parked aft on the fantail, the empennage stuck well beyond the flight deck edge. *Guess I won't be doing a look down the tailpipe, oh well.* There was little to see, with no moon, and no more than the faint glow of my red flashlight. The thick dark gloom of midnight, at sea, smothered vision like blindness. *Bet there's better light in a cow's belly,* I thought. Wishing I could visually check over my aircraft more thoroughly, I put my trust in my teenage plane captain's professionalism, and climbed aboard. Up the ladder, into the cockpit, strapped into the ejection seat and canopy closed. It felt better already, as I settled in organizing charts and checklists.

"START YOUR ENGINES," the voice of the Air Boss belched the loud piercing command, from his tower, high above the deck. Aircraft came to life and the eerie calm was broken. We began to tilt sharply to starboard as the 90,000-ton carrier began its hard turn to port, hunting for the prevailing wind for launch. A formation of butterflies took flight in my belly, as last checks for take-off were completed. With wheel chocks removed, flight deck director's lighted yellow wands guided me and my Skyhawk toward a bow catapult for hookup and launch. Condensation began to build on the canopy. I could scarcely see the motion of the director's lighted wands as I followed his guidance. Straining to see, I eased throttle forward. The aircraft moved slowly up the deck toward the "cat," like a reluctant child contemplating a wild carnival ride. *Best disregard thought of ship's movement and the strong winds gusting over the deck,* I reminded myself. Paramount at this moment was getting proper hook-up to the catapult.

Experience had taught how critically unforgiving carrier flight operations can be. The aircraft buffeted while maneuvering, with wheel brakes and pivoting nose wheel, to accomplish connection with the catapult shuttle. Achieving successful flying speed required the hook-up be done one way – the RIGHT way! Puffs of steam snarled up, from the catapult track, as if daring the next pilot to take a ride.

Hooked up with the engine churning at maximum-power, I had the takeoff checklist completed. The catapult officer took charge, watching for my signal to go. My anxious eyes scanned the instruments one last time: OIL PRESSURE-OK, ENGINE RPM-100%, TAILPIPE TEMPERATURE-Red Hot, GENERATOR- 'Putting out sparks,' MAGNETIC COMPASS-Checked, DIRECTIONAL GYRO-Set and Checked, GYRO HORIZON-Erect, EJECTION SEAT-Armed and Ready. *Go for launch,* I gulped, as I flicked external running lights on, the pilot's signal to fire the catapult. Mind focused, body braced, muscles tensed; a thrust of steam from the "catshot" propelled Skyhawk down the catapult track from zero to flying speed in two seconds! Vision narrowed during acceleration, as the "g" force enraptured me. Grasping the control stick gently, I flew up and away from the carrier. Eyeballs stuck to flight instruments as if by glue. The "bird" and I nosed upward as we blasted through multiple cloud layers; first scud, then cumulus and finally silky stratus cloud layers.

Blackness was intense and everywhere. Night got darker by the second. Breathing and heart-rate had no time to calm when bright flashes lit the cockpit like a mini-explosion! *Saint Elmo's Fire*...phenomenon that seldom occurs at sea, suddenly livened up Mother Nature's evening performance. Atmospheric conditions, a combination of static electricity, humidity and air pressure, created rapidly striking flashes of brilliant light. *Fourth of July sparklers,* I thought, as the flashes bounced off the cockpit bulletproof windscreen into my face. The continuous stream of miniature "lightning bolts" ruined night vision and disrupted my concentration, causing moments of confusion. No! No! Vertigo! I tried desperately to maintain my scan on the cockpit instrumentation, believing what the gauges were telling me. Though my instruments told me I was flying straight — wings level — nose up, I felt convinced I was rolling left in a steep dive. Fighting temptation to *go with seat of the pants,* I disregarded false sensations. Vertigo had held me in its grip times before, but never quite so dramatically. *Stay with it,* I told myself over and over. *It can't last much longer,* I reassured myself, straining at it both mentally and physically, *I can gut this out!*

Just then, Skyhawk broke clear on top of a layer of puffy cotton-like clouds. "It's NOT a moonless night after all," I blared on the radio to my squadron-mates, still climbing out below me. A full moon smiled so brightly it lit the night like downtown Manhattan. Countless twinkling stars filled the sky with beauty, doing their part to brighten the show. *Nature had outdone itself decorating for this midnight party,* I thought, as things in my head returned to normal. Wingmen completed their rendezvous joining, on my right, in smart echelon formation. Four Skyhawk drivers headed off into the clear night sky to complete their assigned mission. Visual flight conditions gave us time to relax and calm our heart rates. I squeezed perspiration from my soaked flight gloves thinking, *No sweat!* Nearly an hour remained to talk with the moon, count stars and enjoy! Then it was back down through the clouds for a moonless carrier landing on board USS Saratoga, floating in cover of darkness somewhere in the Mediterranean Sea.

That's how I remember it.

LOW FUEL

There I was at 3,000 feet in orbit overhead USS Saratoga with a number of aircraft from my squadron. We awaited call-back to the aircraft carrier landing pattern. It being my first-ever **night** carrier landing qualification attempt, I was somewhat apprehensive. I had proven my ability to land safely on the carrier deck in daylight a few days prior. My highly anticipated opportunity to achieve qualification to land jet aircraft, **after dark**, had finally arrived.

Flying an approach for "recovery," as it was called, aboard a rapidly moving vessel at sea, on a black night with no lights, was a challenge. Some seasoned pilots, in my squadron, had logged night landings many times previously. I was a rookie experiencing the thrill of night carrier operations for the first time. Hoping I would be at the top of my game, I felt the anxiety I'd heard about. My job was to keep it under control.

My "ride" was an A4 Skyhawk attack bomber; single engine, single piloted, with an approach airspeed of 115 knots (nautical miles per hour). "Sara," our pet name for USS Saratoga, maintained speed, as necessary, to provide 25-knots of wind over the deck. Aircraft "closure rate" at touchdown was 90 knots (near 100 miles per hour), pretty fast, at night with limited range of vision. Flying an approach demands nothing less than your best effort — full attention to detail! At night you try even harder.

We had been ordered to clear the landing pattern while Sara's crew worked feverishly to repair an arresting gear problem. Delays didn't happen often, on deck, but this time a reliable piece of equipment failed. The Air Boss wasn't giving much information on the radio, except reminders that orbiting pilots must *conserve* precious fuel remaining. I had the lowest amount of fuel remaining of the five orbiting aircraft. My aircraft was to be refueled on deck following the next arrested landing.

I'd had "OKAY PASSES" on my first two arrestments. I needed six to qualify. Then trouble occurred on the flight deck. *These damn things don't happen often, so why are they happening on my watch?* I mumbled. Sure don't like what's going on down there. I feared the waiting and wondering might negatively affect the quality of my next approaches. I grew impatient while waiting. I knew that wasn't a good thing. *Just got to remain calm,* I coached myself.

As orbiting continued, my mind began to search for things to worry about: *It's getting darker and I can no longer see the horizon* (and important visual reference during night flight). *My fuel quantity is dropping fast. I hope I don't screw up my next approach. Are they EVER going to get this problem fixed, or are we done for the night?* I was losing my power of positive thinking. My "right stuff" seemed to be starting to slip away.

Then, dreaded word crackled over my radio. I heard my call sign, *"Atombuster - 507," you're at 'bingo fuel.'"*

Instructions from the Air Boss followed. I was told to divert to land-base Cuba for refueling, then standby for call-back to continue carrier landing qualifications.

My heart sank. I was feeling serious fatigue after a full day of training flights over land, and now night carrier flight operations. I had been feeling high confidence that I would refuel on deck, between landings, and continue qualifying. That was not going to happen. While the other squadron pilots continued to orbit overhead Sara, I departed as directed.

With the carrier cruising majestically in the Caribbean Sea, 100 nautical miles south of US Naval Base Guantanamo Bay, Cuba, with its "fouled" flight deck, I reluctantly climbed while heading northbound for Gitmo. Sara's Air Operations radioed, *"Atombuster - 507, Range and bearing to Guantanamo - 355 degrees, 97 nautical miles."* I acknowledged. My aircraft navigation equipment continued to spin with no lock-on for Gitmo; not a good thing. I reverted to dead-reckoning (DR) navigation using the information passed to me from Sara. Cruising at airspeed of 300-knots, I calculated 20 minutes flight time to Gitmo, with little fuel to spare. Negative things were beginning to bunch-up: navigation malfunction, low fuel remaining and a hunt in the dark for a place to land. Perhaps I HAD misreported my fuel remaining a tad, hoping to remain in orbit until flight deck repairs were made so I could refuel onboard Sara.

It came time to request divine intervention: *Help me stretch my scant remaining fuel. Spare me from shark-infested waters below. Show me Guantanamo — quickly!"* Actually…I was pleading. As darkness continued to thicken, there were no lights in sight. I proceeded northbound straining to pick up the naval base's rotating beacon. *Was I staring too hard?* My eyes felt like they were piercing into a black bowling ball. I saw nothing, absolutely nothing.

Navy A4 Skyhawk getting arrested on flight deck of USS Saratoga, CVA-60, with, Jim, Attack Squadron - 36, at the controls, getting warmed up for night qualifications in waters south of Cuba, it's 1959.

Suddenly, I observed flickering lights below my aircraft. I was flying over land, not water! In darkness, I had reached landfall and was definitely NOT where I wanted to be. I was, instead, over Cuban countryside. That made Skyhawk 507 fair game for hostile fire. The only part of Cuba authorized for over-flight was the area inside the fenced perimeter of US Naval Base at Guantanamo. My DR navigation had obviously taken me off course. I was lost over Cuba and about to flameout from fuel starvation.

Yanking back on the control stick, I added power, disregarding lack of fuel. A major lesson taught in basic pilot training was: *When lost - REMEMBER 3-Cs: CLIMB, CONFESS, CONSERVE.* I climbed to gain better communications reception and visibility while calling Gitmo's Control Tower to confess. Surprisingly, I received a prompt reply. Explaining that I was unsure of my position (lost), I requested tower's guidance to Gitmo's duty runway. Tower confirmed my position with steering to base. I reversed course while regaining hope.

In moments, I cleared a mountain ridge east of the field. The sight of a lighted runway was like a warm hug. It was a thing of beauty. Lowering wheels and flaps, I banked sharply for line-up and touchdown. I savored my survival as the engine continued to put out thrust. As my wheels kissed the asphalt runway, I thanked my savior — that Navy flight controller on duty in the control tower.

Midnight had passed, it was now well into April 30, 1959. I had survived my ordeal. The engine continued to run so I requested taxi clearance back to the squadron flight line. My fuel quantity indicator read empty. Coincidentally, Sara sent all orbiting aircraft back to Gitmo that night as the problem didn't get resolved. I debriefed, headed to the barracks, flopped into my rack and slept like a rock.

Next morning, after further review, it was determined Skyhawk 507 had 15 degrees of magnetic compass error caused by steel structure interference while operating on the carrier's flight deck. I apparently had neglected to manually reset my compass heading while catapulting during landing qualifications. Erroneous headings and faulty navigation had caused illegal over-flight of Cuba. The violation was never reported, thankfully. Further, my aircraft fuel quantity indicator had given erroneous reading; fortunately they had been in my favor. My request for divine intervention had been heard and granted.

Night landing qualifications were completed onboard Sara the next night without incident. I had no further "LOW FUEL" episodes; no more climb, conserve and confess scenarios, during my 16 years of Navy flying that followed. I learned my lessons well that frightful night.

That's how I remember it.

GETTING ARRESTED

It was my only way to get back home. Arriving felt like being jerked up short. It was exhilarating! Getting arrested on board a Navy ship was something to be proud of when things went well.

Arrestments were recorded on video and later, entered into the pages of the pilot's flight log book. In the squadron's ready room carrier arrestments were displayed on the "greenie" board, conspicuously and in color by the pilot's name. Green signified a good landing, black meant an average pass and red meant *you were dangerous!* Getting arrested was routine during aircraft carrier flight operations. You couldn't get back home any other way.

Navy aircraft carriers were home away from home when cruising at sea. The carrier was code-named "home plate," colored hazy gray, and usually underway, with its 1,000 foot-long flight deck, four powerful steam catapults used for takeoffs, and four steel arresting cables used for landings. The mammoth carriers were floating airfields. Deployments often lasted for many months while families stayed behind to fend for themselves and to worry. Pilots rated a stateroom, usually shared with another pilot of equivalent rank. Collateral duties were assigned in the squadron but flying was the pilot's purpose in being on board. Several thousand crew members were onboard the carrier to support flight operations. The carrier's sole purpose was to launch attack missions against the enemy when called upon.

* * * * *

Landing on an aircraft carrier was and still is a rather unique occupation, one which only accepts volunteers. It all had to start somewhere for me and it wasn't in the agricultural paradise of my home state of South Dakota. Rather, it was on a small and lonely unmanned practice landing strip surrounded by farmers' fields in southern Alabama. The asphalt landing area was painted to simulate the look of a carrier deck. We trained to hit our touchdown spot precisely on every landing approach. There was no forgiveness for missing the mark.

Four months after his solo flight, Jim qualified on USS Saipan, a straight-deck,
World War II light aircraft carrier, in the Gulf of Mexico, with six arrested landings
in the SNJ Texan and a lot of extra heartbeats. A Navy press release with this photo in
The Estelline Journal, August 1956, tells the news back home.

Daily, for two weeks in August 1956, just after dawn when the prevailing wind conditions were fairly calm, I flew my Texan trainer from the main air station to the practice strip. I entered the FCLP (field carrier landing practice) pattern to commence grinding out touch and go landings under the close scrutiny of my flight instructor who was on deck with his LSO (Landing Signal Officer) paddles watching my every move. "Paddles" was the handle given to pilots who volunteered their time and expertise in waving, grading and critiquing airplane drivers as they made their approaches for landing on the carrier, by day, at night and in all types of weather.

My instructions were to closely observe the LSO's colorful hand-held paddles as he waved each of my approaches. When the LSO's paddles were held up, it meant I was too high, when he held them down, I was too low, when he pumped them together, it meant I needed to add power (throttle), when he pumped the paddles anxiously, it meant I needed to add lots of power, IMMEDIATELY. Paddles also had a radio for communicating with the pilots in the landing pattern. He rarely talked, unless it was to chew someone out for mistakes being made in their approach.

There were five student pilots in my flight. We struggled together day after day, working to improve our skills so that one day we could successfully qualify as Navy carrier pilots. My progress in pilot training had been okay. Now it was time to demonstrate competence in flying a low, slow power approach to a precision touchdown exactly at the desired spot in the landing area on deck. After logging 60 grueling FCLP approaches, I was cleared to qualify on the carrier. Surprised was an understatement when I was told, "You're good to go!" I rationalized, "Gee, if gruff old Lieutenant Commander Kramp thinks I'm ready—I must be!"

We flew back to the main air station in formation as all five of us received clearance to attempt qualification that morning. We exchanged our Texans for the model with a tail hook installed. At this point, hope was running high; we would soon be getting arrested on the carrier. Just the thought of what we were about to do was exciting however there was apprehension which I suppressed by telling myself I could and must do this. It would be a bit scary, I'd heard the talk. With 120 pilot hours, half of them with an instructor also in the cockpit, I was now about to try getting arrested, solo! I needed six arrested landings to qualify.

Six yellow Texan trainers, equipped with tailhooks, joined in formation, following LCDR Kramp, our LSO instructor and flight leader. We stayed on his wing as he headed into the Gulf of Mexico in search of USS Saipan. She was a World War II aircraft carrier, now being utilized as the ready deck for student pilots in training from the Navy's basic training command, at Pensacola, Florida.

During carrier training phase, I had completed 13 hours of flying time and learned the tricks of the trade for carrier landing qualification. It was an exciting time in my short flying career. Next up was the opportunity to prove myself. Every pilot in naval aviation was required to carrier qualify before receiving Wings of Gold. Even student pilots heading for advanced training in land-based multi-engine aircraft or other non-carrier based aircraft assignments had to qualify on the carrier. The requirement were simple, either carrier qualify and move on, or fail and be dropped from pilot training.

The day's weather could not have been better it was CAVU (ceiling and visibility unlimited). USS Saipan quickly came into view sailing under a beautiful blue sky with a calm sea. Without delay, we were called down into the landing pattern to commence making arrested landings. I was first in the flight to try my luck. The carrier deck was clear, not another aircraft in sight. I was the subject of everyone's attention. I made my approach as I had practiced on land, but I noticed the ship was moving away from me, it was underway at about 20 knots (nautical miles per hour). It seemed to take a few extra seconds to catch up with the spot on the deck where I intended to land. I got the cut-throttle signal from the LSO and landed. *"WOW, that wasn't so tough,"* I quietly exclaimed to myself as I prepared for more.

Raising the tail hook lever to release the arresting cable, I taxied forward to realign for a deck launch takeoff. Adding full power caused my Texan to accelerate down the flight deck like a happy bird with a stolen big fat worm. Five more successful carrier landings followed and I was finished. It took much less time than I had expected. In less than an hour, the whole flight was qualified and heading inbound to the naval base. It was different from the flight outbound, our heads were now bigger, our helmets were a bit tighter—we were now qualified Navy carrier pilots. We had been arrested!

That's how I remember it.

EMOTIONS

All is secure for April at home in Poquott, New York, at 18 White Pine Lane.

SAFE HOME

"She needs a safe home? What do you mean by that?" I asked.

"She needs someone to care for her in a safe place. She needs protection from her parents who reportedly are neglectful and abusive. She needs care quickly! We're speaking about an infant who is basically helpless. It'll be for a short while, perhaps only two, or three months. I can do this. We can do this. Don't you think?"

My wife, Bente, spoke in an unusually assertive tone.

Thus began an adventure that was far more challenging than we could ever have imagined. We were ages 48 and 61. Approaching retirement and close to Social Security eligibility, I was the "old one." Our children: Kim, Robin, James and David were grown and out of the house. There was space available in our five-bedroom home.

How could we not take in an infant for a short while who needed an escape from harm's way? My mind was busy mulling over what so doing might do to our routine; what it might do to our marriage and my fast approaching retirement. Then it happened!

Baby April was flown up from Florida and dropped off at our house by her father who had recently gained custody after separating from April's mother. He left his infant daughter with us on March 31, 1994, one day prior to her first birthday. The "Tot Dad" provided us with one small bag of baby clothes and a handwritten Power of Attorney note granting authority to approve medical treatment for April, in case of an emergency "while she was on her visit." He departed abruptly. That day was her last contact with either of her birth parents. Her mother disappeared. She has made no effort to check-in, or connect, with her daughter since April's safe home landing in 1994. Though we didn't realize it at the time, we had become April's only family. We were first made aware of the need for this "mission of mercy" by Bente's mother who had done private nursing duty, some years earlier, for the family well before April was born.

Getting acquainted happened quickly as we showed April her spacious playpen, comfy crib and decorated nursery, with sunlight shining in and a great view looking out. We introduced her to our pets, a dog and two cats,

*Jim holds April as Gram Roth welcomes the
new addition to her life with the Roths, March 31, 1994.*

and to a new and better life style. April was plump, she appeared to be well nourished. She was a good eater, but we did have some concerns.

Her head was miss-shaped, flat on the backside, perhaps from long hours of cradling, in a baby carrier, while staring endlessly at television. April's baby bottle was her close companion, but that need soon disappeared. She showed little emotion other than her occasional, but surprising and rather strange, fear of males. She was unable to stand without assistance, creep or rollover. It was fairly obvious that the early days of her childhood had been void of stimulation, attention and parental love. Initially, we suspected that April may have some degree of retardation. What have we gotten ourselves into? We pondered.

Within a relatively short period, we observed more enthusiasm, from our new baby. April's sweet smile beamed quite often, her nap time was more relaxed and some nice traces of personality began to emerge. She found comfort in her newly discovered surroundings; good smells, pleasant sounds, frequent hugs, squeezes and unbounded love. Her random "night-frights" accompanied by uncontrollable crying episodes broke the still of the night occasionally, but gradually the spells began to disappear. It took awhile.

Guardedly, April began to creep and to hesitantly stand alone. Finally, she took her solo and triumphant first steps at 19 months of age. It was some time later that we learned of her spinal injury, at four months of age, due to abuse. She had endured convulsions, from abusive smothering, at about the same time. At age two, April was like a fish in our pool, she learned to swim by age three. Her swim stroke was a bit unorthodox, but she had no fear of water, enjoying underwater swims as much as those on the surface. April bonded quickly with family members, neighbors and friends. Her pretty smile and developing sweetness brightened the day for those around her. She had developed into a happy child.

So soon, it seemed, she was off to pre-school, summer camp and then kindergarten, in a private school, requiring students to wear uniforms. April loved school, the bus ride, her uniforms, classroom activities, as well as the excitement of being with kids her age, something we were unable to provide.

Prior to entering public school, her evaluations revealed difficulties with reading and concerns related to attention deficit, as well as her below average intelligence quotient. Some added educational services were arranged for April, as she began first grade.

April became a reader early in her first year of public school, surprising everyone including herself. She was pleased. We were proud. However, by the end of third grade an academic struggle had begun. Our level of concern grew as she gradually dropped further behind, in spite of her hard work. April's love of school and her excellent attendance record continued, but frustration began to show and discipline problems arose both at home and in school.

In fourth grade, April was moved to an "inclusion classroom" where she received normal classroom instruction supplemented by additional services provided for by special education teachers. The adjustment was instantly successful for April and her level of achievement improved dramatically. Inclusion continued, through her years of junior high school. The goal for April to achieve, an upgraded, New York State Regents diploma, from secondary school, continued on track. Her weakness in math still plagued her, until Sylvan Learning Center entered her life. Comprehensive test batteries revealed a two-year deficit, in her math grade-level skills, as well as some deficiency in reading/writing. With Sylvan's guarantee to help April, she was enrolled for remedial help in both areas. She has continued at Sylvan, four-hours weekly since. Math has become her favorite and strongest subject. As a high school tenth grader, April's performance continues at grade-level and on track for Regents diploma accomplishment. Her school staff, family and friends take pride in how hard she works to be all that she can be. The wearing of a Ward Melville High School, 2011 Class ring, gives her added incentive to complete her success story.

There have been some "bumps" getting to this point. April, however, has "good survivor instincts" and strong determination. She has hit it lucky along life's way, particularly with the assistance of enthusiastic teachers and loyal friends who collectively and willingly go that extra mile to assist and advise her.

Her Roth brothers and sisters have always been supportive. April knows she is a "true member" of the family, even with her different last name. April's safe home presence has made it a better place for everyone. We are happy she came to live with us—15 years ago.

That's how I remember it.

APRIL FIRST

All alone is when no one wants me. I am a baby girl lost in a big world and don't realize it because I am very small. Being one-year-old, my father in prison and my mother gone, is a predicament. My brother, just a bit older, was hospitalized with injuries from abuse. I'm not sure where he is. No one in my family wants to help.

Wait, what's this? I am taken in by a family who has given me a home! My new crib, room with a view, toys, tasty food, clean clothes and nice warm baths feel so good. Nice people hold me, talk to me and stroll with me. Suddenly I don't feel so alone. Look, I can roll over, crawl and reach for things. Smiling is fun. I'm going to do it more often. I like all the good smells. I like it — being picked up and held lovingly is new to me. The pets roam past my play pen to investigate, sometimes stopping to sniff, or to give me a lick. They are checking out their new competition, but I feel secure.

The bad days have ended; no more screaming, shouting, hitting or hurting. I won't be smothered again, or tossed from a balcony like a ball. No one will step on me, squeeze me harmfully, or abuse and violate me in places that don't feel good. I'm safe for the first time. I like it here because it seems that...*April comes first!*

Days pass quickly and I enjoy each one. I can stand alone. Diapers get changed often; they are comfortable and don't get heavy, or smelly. I eat a lot and am growing fast. My sleep is good in my own quiet room. I love long walks in my stroller. Everyone I see is friendly; they talk to me and smile. I am beginning to understand what they are saying.

I get many new toys and play things. The family room with my big toy box is my favorite place to play. It took a long while, but I'm finally walking and talking, after 19 months. I make my family laugh with some of my antics. I am a bit shaky when I walk and I lisp when I talk, but no one seems to mind. I am going to stay here a long, long time — I hope.

I call her Bente; I think she is my Mom. I call him Jim; I think he is my Dad. It doesn't matter because I love them and I know they love me. I call this college guy, Dave. I think he's my brother; maybe he's my uncle. I hear Katie calling him, "Uncle Dave." I like Katie. She's more than twice

When April and Katie swim together,
April enjoys the company and Katie enjoys giving the lessons.

April, Mom Bente and Nelson DeMille share a smile at OHEKA Castle after he notes in and signs her book, OHEKA CASTLE Monument to Survival, a book about April's ancestry.

April loves Dave. When they have some time together she lights up a smile.

my age, but always lots of fun. It's the strangest thing, how she calls Jim, "Grandpa." I call him that too when Katie is here. Jim doesn't mind what I call him. You will see me light up when I'm with Dave and Katie. I love them very much.

A big day happens — I'm really glad! No more diapering, or accidents in my pants. It's nice to have that over. Jim and Bente are proud of me. They liked the way I said, "That's it!" My clothes fit better; it's easier for me to dress myself. I like this feeling of freedom. Best of all, my swim suit fits right and getting out of the pool to go potty is something I can handle quite well now. I like doing things for myself. There are problems going to the toilet alone, but I'm learning to deal with it. Jim and Bente enjoy my new-found skill. They give me lots of encouragement and praise.

I like learning new things. I get lots of help and have learned to set the table, strap myself into the car seat, use the handrail on the stairs, flush the toilet, wash my hair, dress myself, brush my teeth, pickup, cleanup, lock the door, and more. Bente teaches me about colors, flowers, letters and reading. Jim teaches me to swim, dive and to hold my breath under water. He takes me boating, fishing, walking and into the yard to work with him. I lose interest in yard work quickly. I love learning; I hope it never stops.

What's this yellow thing sitting in our driveway? It's a school bus with kids on board and a seat for me! Off I go to Laurel Hill for pre-school, with a teacher by the name of Mrs. Love. Can it get any better than this? I don't see how! There are many playmates in school. This, Jim and Bente did not provide for me at home. I have to learn quickly to share, to be kind to others and to stop screaming.

I decided I had to start calling Jim and Bente, "Dad" and "Mom," cause that's what the other kids call their parents. I have loved school since that first day. I am sad when I am sick and have to stay home. I get anxious for vacations to end so I can get back on my little yellow school bus. Two years of pre-school and two summers at Laurel Hill Camp have helped me get my act together. In the fall, I will be starting kindergarten. I hear it is much harder than pre-school. I want to be ready. I am working hard on my letters, numbers, coloring, singing, dancing, and artistic stuff, as well as my "getting-along" skills so that I will be able to make it in kindergarten. Mom and Dad want me to be a good student. They work with me a lot. I think I want to grow up to be a nurse, or maybe a doctor.

As I grow, I'm learning to swing a golf club and to strum my guitar. I love the fun of fiddling with the VCR and TV controls. I feed the pheasants and wild birds, in our back yard, ride my tricycle, let the dog in and out, pick up my things, and do many other helpful chores. I am big for my age. People think I am six, or even older. I will be only five, on my birthday. I think it will be the best ever! I try to do my jobs well and be good. Things work out best when I stay out of trouble. Mom and Dad have given me a nice place to live and grow up. I am lucky they came along when they did! I wonder where I'd be now if I hadn't gotten lucky and caught up in their care. It's been fun growing up where I live because…April comes first!

That's how April remembers it.

Epilogue:

April, born on April 1st, is now 16 years-of-age and in 10th grade. She is nearly on the honor roll and she participates her high school bowling and golf teams. Out of respect, we make no jokes on April Fools' Day. April's birth father died of cancer on May 10, 2008. Her birth mother has never been located; April has not had contact with her birth parents since her "safe home" arrival on March 31, 1994. She has recently initiated limited contact with her paternal grandmother residing in Kansas.

TURNING SIXTY

I was feeling great — happy to have made it to sixty; growing older seemed to be "no sweat." Mom was a loving mother, but she kept asking a nagging question.

"Jim, have you had a physical exam lately? I really wish you would have that done. It would be for me, you know."

She would bring up the topic, occasionally, when we talked on the phone. Mom had contributed greatly to my good health by the mothering she did while I was growing up in Estelline, South Dakota. Having lost my brother, Bill, at age 36, from cancer, and having just recently lost my Dad, also from cancer, Mom didn't want to take any chances on losing me. She had a good point.

"Sure, Mom, I'll get to it one day," was always my response.

It seemed the least I could do to help keep Mom happy and free from worry. Since my Navy retirement, I'd pretty much taken my good health for granted. I had no family doctor, so I asked around. Post birthday, especially for Mom who hardly ever asked me for anything, I finally arranged to see a local physician for a "well physical," I called it.

It went well: EKG — good, blood pressure — excellent, blood drawn — with a small prick, urine sample — dribbled into a cup, flu shot — injected, and so on until I was directed to the receptionist for check-out. During my military flying career it was routine to have a comprehensive physical examination annually. *This was so simple,* I was thinking.

Several days passed, then came the surprise phone call from my doctor's office. His nurse greeted, "Hello, Commander Roth, I've called to advise that Dr. Kornrich would like you to see your urologist. Your PSA (prostate specific antigen) lab test score came back slightly elevated."

"Okay. Do you have anyone in the area that you'd recommend?" I replied, much preferring that I could be talking to my doctor directly.

A momentary pang of anxiety struck as I waited her response. She gave me a name. I thanked her and hung up. The ordeal had begun. First there was the ten-day wait for an appointment, followed by discussion with the urologist about what to do next. I endured the unpleasantness of the transrectal ultrasound exam and biopsy he administered. Another long week passed while awaiting the lab report. When the doctor's office called, I had hopes for some good news about the biopsy. Instead, I was directed to return for another doctor's visit. My level of concern was now spiked. At a follow-up appointment, one week later, I heard the shocking news.

"Jim, I certainly didn't think I would be telling you this, but...you do have prostate cancer."

I left the doctor's office, headed straight for Radiology, for further examination: CAT scan and bone scan. My mind was numb. After the scans were completed, I headed home, struggling with how best to inform my family of such dreadfully bad news.

The good life was rapidly turning to crap right before my eyes. I thought, "Why me?" The news must have been devastating to my wife, but she gave her best effort to remain positive. I promptly wrote a letter to Mom, who lived alone in a distant city. She screamed aloud as she read my letter, which was carefully crafted with the best "wordsmith skills" I could employ. Mom was inconsolable. She immediately called my daughter, Kim, who lived nearby, breaking the news to her between outbursts of tears. They tried to console each other and to find a positive thought regarding the development. It wasn't an easy time.

Coincidentally, while mentally preoccupied and stumbling along in the passageway coming out of radiology, I happened to notice a prostate cancer support group meeting announcement on the clinic bulletin board. For the next two months, I faithfully attended the group meeting weekly, listening to similarly afflicted men tell stories of their choices, treatments and results. So doing helped me chart my course of action.

I sought a second opinion from Zelik Frischer, MD, Professor of Urology, at Long Island's Stony Brook University Hospital, who had been recommended to me by the prostate cancer support group leader. During our first consultation with the doctor, Bente and I agreed on which treatment seemed best. Having made the decision on choice of treatment gave some relief, but only briefly. I began mentally preparing for surgery and banking my blood in readiness for going "under the knife." The limited availability of surgical suites was frustrating; I wanted action and quickly. Because I agreed to a day that was unpopular in the minds of many patients, I received my surgery schedule date promptly.

On Friday the 13th of February, 1993, in pre-dawn darkness, Bente drove the two of us to the hospital. While we traveled the 40-minute trip, conversation was limited. We both knew and felt the serious nature of the situation. While my check-in was being handled, I passed my valuables to Bente with a hug and kiss. Leaving my clothes behind, away I went with a surgical staff expediter heading me off to "market" on a shiny silver gurney.

Struggling to look and act brave, I gave my best effort to appear ready for anything they could throw at me. I was wide awake when rolled into the surgery suite where rows of instruments of all sizes and shapes awaited a crack at my body. Medical staff swarmed about, preparing for my "fix" which was to be observed by a gallery of aspiring medical students.

The attempt to inject the over-sized needle for my "spinal" didn't go well. The decision was quickly made to alter course and to put me to sleep intravenously. At this point, I could have cared less. "Just put me out, I can't stand the glare," I tried to mumble. Quickly, I was absorbed by the safe arms of "deep slumber."

Much later, I was never told the time it took to complete the procedure, I awoke in my hospital room. My eyes opened slowly and guardedly to the sight of tubes running, into and out of my body, from various locations. I felt no pain, but I knew I had been revamped. I didn't know to what extent. Eventually, my surgeon arrived bedside. Speaking in a positive tone of voice, he gave me his word that all had gone well. I heard him say it, "You are cancer free!" Dr. Frischer was smiling, as he spoke the best news I'd heard in months.

Badly scarred by a "near foot and a half long incision," running down my front side, I had missing body parts. It was the "cancer free" words that stuck in my mind; everything else seemed secondary at the moment. I grew a bit anxious, as the days passed, waiting for my systems to resume normal body function. After clearing those hurdles, I was good to go. It had taken me five days to get my body totally untraumatized.

The medical staff prepared me to head back to the comforts of home. They insisted I depart with a piece of their medical apparatus still installed. I was "granted" a clumsy catheter system with see-through urine collection bag strapped to my leg. Oh well, anything to get back home.

For two weeks, though it seemed much longer, I tolerated the ugliness of the catheter; it was a necessary step in my recovery. Once it was removed, I became aware of another problem; a seriously leaky "valve!" I fixed it, over time. A lengthy do-it-yourself project that turned out to be.

After a five-week rehabilitation period at home, I went back to work, leading my Riverhead High School Navy NJROTC Corps of Cadets. Recovery took patience and understanding, but it went well. I timed my bathroom visits, once every hour, as I slowly regained control of things. The peeing in my pants had to stop, and eventually it did.

I was thankful there was no post-surgery treatment required and that I was able to regained control of my life. Getting completely healed and back in ship-shape was an effort. I will always be mindful of Mom's insistence on getting that physical exam. Her persistence saved my life, perhaps. I had no idea I was in harm's way, until the PSA test, during my "well" physical exam, started this chain of events. Nine months passed before a feeling of total well-being returned. That was 16 years ago. I felt "born again" in a physical way. I was cancer-free. I am cancer-free!

That's how I remember it.

CRISIS STRUCK

I looked up; there stood Bente. Strange, I thought, how did she locate me here? I was at the marina where we kept our runabout, doing some cleaning. It was a location that she had never laid eyes on. Why she had come to find me was baffling.

"I thought you were going to get gas in my car," she remarked.

"That's my next 'honey-do'...I'll stop for a fill-up soon as I finish polishing off the boat."

"We have to go to the Brookhaven Hospital...right now...David has been injured in a swimming pool accident." Barely coherent, she'd lost color in her face.

"How bad is it?" I asked, not knowing for sure if I really wanted to hear her reply.

She began to sob and said nothing more. Quickly securing the cleaning gear, we began a fast-walk toward the cars, both fearing the worst.

"Let's take my car, it has a full tank."

Now...wanting to know more, I tried to continue our dialogue without increasing Bente's level of panic. Searching delicately for the right words, I asked for more details. She explained that the call from Brookhaven Hospital's emergency room was calm and compassionate. The nurse had said that our son arrived by ambulance with a neck injury.

By this time, we were on the road and discussing which would be the best and quickest route to take to Brookhaven Hospital. Bente repeated to me what the nurse had said on the phone.

"He was conscious, stable and able to move his limbs." Using language filled with encouragement, she attempted to soften the shock of her news. The nurse continued.

"This is not a life-threatening injury, so please drive carefully. He didn't want me to call you, but I'm also a Mom."

Twenty-five miles of driving to the Brookhaven Hospital seemed never ending. Our sense of urgency to be at Dave's bedside kept the pedal to the metal...*speeding ticket be damned!*

We fell silent, each struggling with our own fear while endless possible scenarios flashed through our minds. Our talk resumed as we approached the hospital parking area.

"We've probably set a speed record, but it seems to have taken us forever! Now where do we park?" I saw no open space.

"Drop me off at the emergency entrance," Bente requested. Just then a "Reserved for Doctors" parking space opened up; I swung into it and stopped.

Parking illegally didn't seem to matter at this critical moment. We rushed hand-in-hand for the entrance to ER. Passing through the tall swinging doors we saw Dave's friends, awaiting our arrival. They appeared anxious and relieved to see us and held the doors as we entered. Four grim-faced young men extended a warm, but silent handshake. We were expecting the worst, but hoping for the best.

Hearing how they had removed Dave from the pool after he apparently struck his head on the bottom after a dive, left us cold. One of them had thought to grab a cell phone and called 911 immediately. EMT's arrived quickly to attend to Dave. He was placed on a board and loaded into the ambulance. It sped off to the Brookhaven Hospital from the summer house in Hampton Bays where the injury had occurred, with Dave's buddies in trail.

Locating Dave quickly, just inside the ER, placed in a neck brace and strapped to a gurney, brought some relief. There was our strong and beautifully tanned 25-year-old son, lying motionless in swim shorts. With heart monitor attached and IV tubes inserted in both arms, he looked traumatized.

I felt a sizeable lump in my throat. Tears ran down my face. A fear of speaking came over me, not knowing just what the right thing to say might be at this point. The need for information ate at my gut, but I knew the poor guy was in no condition to tell his story. By this time his Mom had caught up; we stood over Dave in anguish. Dave opened his eyes, saw us there, wiggled his toes and squeezed our hands. It was wonderful.

Dr. Mullen, the ER doctor on duty, looking young with short-cropped hair and pleasant demeanor, spoke with us. His words and kind manner gave us hope. He was a neurosurgeon specialist, by stroke of good fortune. We asked about transferring our son to Stony Brook University Hospital, nearer to our home and perhaps better equipped to handle this type of injury. While the doctor made some phone calls, the three of us held a quick family conference, deciding to stick with what we had. We were impressed with Dr. Mullen, as was our son. It was the right call.

Dave stayed overnight "boarded" to a gurney in a screened-off section of the ER — awaiting the availability of Intensive Care Unit. For four days, he remained in ICU awaiting the assembly of a special neurological surgery team and an available surgical suite. The wait took its toll on all of us. The prognosis we so anxiously hoped for was worth the waiting.

During the two-hour surgical procedure, our Dave became 'Titanium Man" as a metal reinforcement rod and screws were implanted to repair the damaged vertebrae. While Dave was in recovery, Dr. Mullen spent nearly an hour with us giving an encouraging debrief of the surgical team's successful accomplishment.

After a month of recuperation and rehabilitation, Dave returned to his job and never looked back — except for many follow-up care visits which his surgeon so caringly administered. He was declared a "lucky guy" by the whole medical team. The injury came very close to being a tragedy of much greater magnitude. His "badge of courage" is a three to four inch scar on the front side of his neck.

From the moment his head struck the bottom of the pool, procedure fell into place for Dave. His buddies made good decisions rescuing him from the pool, the ambulance arrived quickly with an extremely competent EMT team that knew exactly what to do, and the nearest hospital was close by.

Thirty minutes time elapsed from Dave's ill-planned dive to his arrival at the emergency room. Amazing! The ER doctor on duty at the hospital where the ambulance crew chose to take Dave, just happened to be a neurosurgeon, one of Long Island medicine's most noted. We've "thanked our lucky stars" many times and are grateful! There is a pause each year, on the anniversary of Dave's accident, for us to once again give thanks.

That's how we remember it.

April hones her golf skills at St. George's Golf and Country Club and goes on to play with her high school team in 2008-2009 seasons.

CHAIN REACTION

"We should get to it pretty soon if you think it's something we can do. Warner told me this week that they will be burning the piles soon, probably next week."

Bill was referring to free fire wood available for the cutting, if we got to it soon enough. I listened to his phone call as I thought over a plan. Bill was a very busy guy, with little free time, so we had to work around his schedule.

"Okay. How about tomorrow morning, early? I'll bring my chain saw and trailer. I'll pick you up along the way, about eight."

"Great. Plan to drop in for some coffee, okay?"

I liked the way the work plan was coming together. We'd get it done before Christmas, only two days away. Replenishing the fire wood supply for Bill was something we wanted to do. It was our holiday treat for his family. Bill was a popular local physician, one we were fortunate to have caring for our families. Ongoing land clearing for new construction left fallen oak trees bulldozed into tangled piles. The wood was available, first come first served, and located near Bill's place. His family had both of their fireplaces blazing most of the time. Helping them replenish their dwindling wood pile was in the spirit of Christmas.

It was a frosty morning with a bit of haze. A light layer of snow covered the work area, but we entered without getting our car stuck. Krag, a relative of my wife, also one of Bill's patients, joined in with another chain saw. We were set to harvest free fire wood. Woodsmen Krag and Bill set to work on one pile while I headed for another. The snarl of chain saw engines would break the quiet calm of the morning. The next sound I heard was the 'clunk' of a new cut log dropping into the trailer. Our operation was underway.

My chain saw, a unique wedding gift to us from Krag and his wife, baulked as I yanked on the pull rope to get it running. *Damn it,* I muttered, *the blasted thing was just in the shop for checkup and sharpening.* With a couple of adjustments, I soon had it cranked and purring. I revved the throttle and placed the whirring blade onto a good size oak for my first cut of the day. Then something terrible happened.

Flashing stars blinded me as I fell to the ground. Stunned but still conscious, I could see my saw sitting near me, running at idle RPM. Wondering who slugged me, I placed a hand up to my face, drawing back a bloodied work glove. I shut down the saw, struggled to my feet and gathered my wits. Staggering a bit, I walked over to find Bill.

Bill and Krag were shocked when they saw me standing before them in a daze. Their expression told it all. Bill's eyes widened; his jaw dropped. Krag asked me what had happened. Bill maintained his composure and quickly took charge.

"Do you have a handkerchief with you?" He asked.

"Yeah, I think so." I struggled to remove my work gloves so I could search my pockets. "I have one, and it's clean."

"Close your eye and cover it. Hold it firmly. Keep your eye closed."

"I'll unhook the trailer. You get in the car. I'll drive us to Central Suffolk Hospital. It's where we're heading!"

I followed his directions and began to wonder just how seriously I'd been injured. I was woozy. My cheek felt numb. My eye and upper teeth on the right side were aching. I felt myself starting to come "unglued." A wave of nausea swept over me. I prepared to do some vomiting. Shock was enveloping me. I knew it was gut-check time and I'd better handle it. I kept querying myself, *what happened? What did I do wrong?*

En route to the hospital we scarcely spoke. Krag followed in his car. As the car warmed, the heat increased my sensitivity to facial pain. I violated doctor's orders by peeking out from under the handkerchief. I had to know if I had vision in my battered eye. Things looked blurred. *Probably from the bleeding,"* I thought. I tried to remain calm.

Although the hospital was but a few miles away, it seemed to take forever to get there. Thoughts flipped through my mind like flash cards: *How wonderful our wedding party had been at the country club near where we had been cutting wood. How exciting the arrival of our new baby, due very soon, was going to be. How my flying career would be finished if my eyesight was damaged. How long would recovery take and who would cover my flying duties at work.* My mind went into overdrive, I couldn't slow it down. Silenced remained in the car. The nausea faded and I no longer felt like I was going to pass out. I think Bill was planning for the scenario once we arrived at the hospital.

As we approached the swinging doors to enter Emergency, Bill became Dr. Bill Tooker, MD. I was loaded onto a gurney and rolled into a surgical suite. While Doctor Bill scrubbed, nurses cleaned up my face a bit. I answered a battery of questions explaining how the chain saw, for some reason, had kicked back, striking my face a violent blow. Apparently, the engine portion of the chain saw had struck hard enough to change forever the appearance of my face. Fortunately, the vicious and unforgiving cutting blade didn't get to me.

My eyelid was split in pieces by the force of the blow. A deep cut above my eyelid and a vertical gash along the right side of my nose added to the bleeding and pain. Nerve damage had apparently occurred in my right facial area; numbness persisted. Calls were placed for a plastic surgeon, while Dr. Bill worked meticulously to rearrange tattered eyelid pieces for stitching.

When it appeared no plastic surgeon was going to be available, Dr. Bill volunteered to do the needed procedure, subject to my approval.

"Jim, I'm pretty good with a needle. Would you like for me to do the suturing? It could be a couple of days before we can get a plastic surgeon here. It's Christmas, they all seem to be out for the holiday."

I had been lying on my back staring at the overhead flood lights for more than an hour. Dr. Bill had been delicately working the loose flaps of torn eyelid skin back into proper order with his surgical tweezers. His calm manner was a comfort. I felt confidence in his skills and accepted his offer.

"Go for it, Bill, let's get it done."

At this point with things well under control and with nothing more he could do to help, Krag wished me well and departed for home. The procedure began. First came Novocain injections, then came suturing. Bill tended to the laceration by my nose before tackling the eyelid repair. I marveled at his skill as he manipulated through the stitching job with a petite needle that I could hardly see or feel. It seemed as if hours had passed since I arrived in ER. Finally, Bill dressed me up with a face full of bandages and I was prepped for checkout. Concern for what my wife's reaction would be when she learned of my accident and saw my messed up face began to build.

On cue, Dr. Bill spoke up.

"Would you like for me to accompany you home? I know Bente is late into her pregnancy. This probably isn't going to help her blood pressure. (Pause) I think it would be a good idea if I did come home with you."

"Good, I'd appreciate that. I'll run you back home later."

Bente was resting when we arrived. We crept slowly up the spiral staircase to the master bedroom. Our arrival startled her. Then she stared at my bandaged face and said, "Now what have you done to yourself?" She was shocked and spoke with a tone of voice quite lacking in sympathy.

Bill spoke up immediately with a professional explanation of what had happened to me. He emphasized how my good luck had avoided more serious facial damage, and had spared my vision.

"Everything will heal in time and Jim will be good as new," he reassured.

Bente took the doctor's report fairly well, seeming somewhat relieved by the time Dr. Bill was prepared to leave us. With my good eye leading the way, I drove Bill home with an apology for our failure to replenish his fire wood pile. He interrupted with a reminder for me to remove my mask of bandages the next morning to expedite healing. I thanked him again, from the bottom of my heart, for his medical skills and friendship. I returned to the woods, hitched up my empty trailer and towed it home, uneventfully.

The stress filled day had wiped me out. Retiring early, I slept well, awakening at first light to anxiously remove bandages for a survey of the damage. It was early, a new day and Christmas Eve, but my face looked like an ugly Halloween mask. Bente, in her overly pregnant condition, needed my help so we were off to the King Kullen store to do some holiday grocery shopping. The store was full of shoppers and the isles were overly crowded with no place to hide. I became a bit self-conscious about my appearance as shoppers either paused to stare at me, or turned away. My swollen, black and blue face with crusted blood and stitches was grotesque.

Dr. Bill's handy work with his suturing was outstanding. My wounds healed rapidly with little scaring. The illusive plastic surgeon wasn't needed and lost out on the job. Ten days of Christmas and New Years leave went by quickly, but they gave me time to heal. I was back to work and in the air by mid-January. Flying Navy acceptance test flights at Grumman, in Tomcat, Prowler and Intruder aircraft involved high altitude profiles. The wearing of an oxygen mask strapped tightly was required. My facial wounds healed well enough to allow pressure on my face with no problem. Even with chain saw scars now a part of me, I considered the near disaster my *Christmas Miracle of 1973.*

That's how I remember it.

MISSED ME

It had been a long flight with a punctual arrival at Islip Airport, New York. Being back in a time zone my body better understood and being able to sleep in my own bed were thoughts that welcomed me home. The visit I'd had with my parents in Phoenix, Arizona, on the Martin Luther King holiday weekend, had been delightful, but much too brief.

The need for snow removal greeted me in the airport's long-term parking lot. Lacking proper tools, my gloved hands cleared away snow and ice sufficient to allow driving safely out of the parking lot. I headed my lumbering Buick station wagon out the gate towards Veteran's Highway heading east toward Riverhead, New York. The darkness was consuming as the headlights struggled to show me the way. The lack of motor vehicle traffic so near the airport was most usual. After traveling less than a mile, I was startled and shaken by a nerve-shattering noise that broke the still of the night. Abruptly, I focused my full attention. **What the hell was that,** I thought. *Hmm...Should I stop to investigate?* I questioned what to do. While quickly thinking it over, I kept driving. Hearing nothing further that was strange, or unusual, I increased speed and cautiously continued driving toward home.

With my ears perked and listening closely, I glued my eyes to the cluster of gauges on the instrument panel. All appeared normal. While swerving the steering wheel back and forth, I tested my brake pedal. *This is strange. It sure was smart of me not to have stopped in that dark and lonely spot to check over the car,* I rationalized. *Did something fly up from the road surface striking the bottom of the Buick — a piece of steel pipe, a muffler, or other debris?* The noise was a hard hit from something metal, I was certain. The Buick lumbered along smoothly while my mind continued to analyze the sound I'd heard.

The incident gave me a frightful scare. I couldn't get the startling noise out of my head. My heart worked to halt its racing. My wits weren't yet completely back to normal. *It wasn't a rock, or anything small, or light weight. It was a serious cracking jolt.* I remained somewhat baffled. With no more noise, or disruption, I uneventfully pulled into our driveway, off Riverside Drive. Grabbing my luggage, I exited and conducted a walk-around inspection looking for damage. In the dark of night, I could see very little so I quickly headed inside out of the cold. *Whatever it was could wait until morning,* I convinced myself with a slight feeling of relief.

After welcome home greetings and hugs, I gave my wife, Bente, details of the Phoenix visit. I briefly added mention of the car noise heard while pulling onto the main road near the airport. I kept it simple. Next morning in daylight, with the fright still fresh in my mind, I looked the car over more closely. Seeing nothing out of the ordinary, I climbed in and drove off to work. Off and on throughout the day, I continued to wonder about the noise I'd heard driving home from the airport.

A month later, I spotted a dent near the driver's side window, while washing off winter's dirt and grim. The indent, just below eye-level, was in the steel pillar between the front and back doors. The blemish was made more visible by the rust formed on the gouged surface. Like a flash, I realized the damage I was looking at had to have been done by the impact of a bullet fired from a high-powered rifle. The slug had struck forcefully and ricocheted, unable to penetrate the steel structure. Had the perpetrator's shot been a few inches more accurate and pierced the window glass, I would most likely have received a mortal head wound. Judging from the spot on the pillar where the bullet struck, had I been driving just a bit slower, the line of fire of a fast-moving bullet could not have missed me.

Realizing that I had been targeted by sniper-fire was extremely disconcerting — to say the least! I thought seriously about what I could, or should do. Bente and I discussed it further. It seemed it would be a waste of time to notify authorities in late February of criminal gunfire that had occurred in January. I imagined the indifference I would most likely have encountered in dealing with law enforcement people. I rehearsed telling the story of my dark night fright near Islip Airport and felt certain the police would show little if any interest. Perhaps I thought wrong.

I suspected who might have been responsible for the sniper fire and it was alarming. *Building a strong case against him would be difficult with no proof or witnesses,* I rationalized. I knew of a delinquent "trigger-finger-happy" teenager who possessed illegal guns. He'd killed birds, pets and perhaps even people. The guy had no respect for the law, or enforcement officers. He craved gunfire and killing. He was a "lose cannon" in society.

My Phoenix travel itinerary was known to him; he knew the car I was driving, my arrival airport, arrival time and my route of travel home. "Billie Bob," aka "Bad Ass," had acquired a nasty reputation. He disrespected authority, resented society and dropped from school while in junior high. His life was troubled and he liked it that way.

"Billie Bob" knew my whereabouts from information accessed from my wife's mother. The woman had hopelessly attempted to help the kid earlier in his youth without success. Employed for years as his guardian, she had repeatedly referred to me as the person who would come punish him when necessary, although I never did so. He grew to hate me over the years for no good reason. She unwittingly failed herself, "Billie Bob" and me with the manner in which she dealt with things. Her actions had serious flaws.

Several months following my scary roadway "fire in the night" incident, "Billie Bob" was apprehended and jailed for other crimes. He was sentenced to serve time in the county jail for multiple offenses. Over time, he had repeatedly threatened my life and the safety of our family. He was skilled at avoiding the law, while flying below the radar, so to speak. He carried weapons, abused his children, used illegal drugs, drove drunk, wrecked cars, injured people and took large amounts of money illegally. Law enforcement and the courts put him away several times for felonious and other crimes. "Billie Bob" was incarcerated, on and off, for 14 ½ years in state and federal prisons. His death occurred nine weeks prior to release from an ongoing sentence, while in custody of the Federal Bureau of Prisons. On May 10, 2008, at age 38, he succumbed to melanoma cancer. "Billie Bob" didn't live to get a second shot at me.

With this life of crime ended, things for me appeared much brighter. I expect no more ugly threats. The scary rifle fire incident's 20th anniversary, January 15, 2009, did *not* go by without notice.

That's how I remember it.

From this...1966, (L to R) Kim, Robin and James II.

THERE WAS A TIME

There was a time when Jim found himself unable to cope. He wasn't out of work, but he wasn't really working. His work was to fly; it had always been the great escape in times of trouble. A request for temporary suspension from flying duty was granted after he let it be known that he was experiencing stress-related vertigo and disorientation during night and instrument flights. As an experienced instructor pilot, with thousands of hours of pilot time, he knew his students in training depended upon his effectiveness for their successful completion of the all-weather attack flight syllabus, as well as their safety. He knew it was his responsibility to remove himself from "harms way" until he could clear his head. Safe flight required complete concentration, an "up attitude" and an aggressive approach to the many split-second decisions required in rapid-fire succession while at the flight controls. Called the "right stuff" — Jim knew he had lost it...for now.

It had happened once before, ten years earlier; he remembered it well. An upset at home over a matter involving an in-law had triggered a similar reaction. It was quickly resolved and within four days he was back flying. This time it was a much larger issue, and he knew it was not going to go away quickly. Without flying Jim had but one choice and that was to tackle his problem head-on and work toward a solution; there would be no escape to the wild blue yonder. The thought of not being able to jump into an aircraft and challenge flight with his personal skills, was scary. The rush of adrenaline, pulling high "g" forces, crew camaraderie...they couldn't help fight off distress this time. Jim must prepare to go it alone.

The marriage was over; irreconcilable differences had done them in. The children were upset and filled with fear of the unknown. The uncertainty of the future filled their minds with questions. "Where would Mom go? Could Dad care for them? Who would cook? Wash their clothes? Help with homework? Get them off to school? Buy them the things they needed? Care for the pets? What would they tell their friends? How could there be a Merry Christmas? What would teachers say when they heard? Should this be kept a secret?"

Jim felt the urgent need to get a grip on himself quickly before trying to console the children. "What was he going to do and how was he going to resolve this crisis," he thought. He knew he must act immediately and positively in order to restore order and calm the children's justifiable fears. Their tears were tearing his heart out, and for a moment he was afraid to speak for fear they would not listen. As he began speaking with his two daughters, ages eight and nine; the right words seemed to come to him. Their tears stopped, but he knew it was not the last of them. He suggested they work together to make some supper and asked for suggestions on the menu. Soon there was a true team effort going in the kitchen; his three-year-old son pitching in by helping set the table. Keeping busy and organized had a wonderful calming effect. The family continued to talk it out as they worked together. *Perhaps they could survive and rediscover happiness as a family of four...without a wife and mother,* Jim thought to himself. Following a rather late supper and as conversation began to dwindle; Jim announced, *"Hey guys, it's past bedtime!"* Everyone scurried off to their beds, but no one slept well that night.

Time worked its magic. Days passed. Adjustments were made. A sense of harmony and teamwork evolved, boosting spirits for everyone. Goals were established, feelings of pride evolved...togetherness emerged. Friends helped out as people began to understand and realize their predicament. In 1966, a single-parent household, with father as the head, was most unusual.

Jim's workdays were longer, but life became bearable again. He resumed flight status and managed to re-arrange his Navy assignment so as to be more adaptable to his situation. A new home in a new neighborhood was located and with that came a new school. It meant challenges for everyone, including making all new friends. The move happened quickly as the family chose new bedrooms, hung curtains, stowed the cupboards, arranged the furniture and established a working routine. It was exhausting, but exciting; it drew the family together ever so tightly. Skeletons from previous closets seemed to disappear. Fear diminished, school grades began to climb and laughter returned home.

Moral support came from Estelline, a long distance from Virginia, by telephone, letters and visits. Jim's Mom and Dad did wonders in coming to the aid of their son and grandchildren. Their time and good deeds given in support were special; it seemed to certify the hardship situation. A few weeks at "Roth Camp," in Estelline, gave everyone something to look for-

April and visiting Granddaughter Katie and April's brother Robert, from Virginia, found happiness together. Robert is 14 months older than April and Katie is like her Big Sis.

ward to each summer. This small place in South Dakota became a special second home for three Roth grandkids badly in need of extra love and attention. Gram and Gramps excelled with their refreshed parenting skills; they hadn't lost the touch. Their help smoothed the turbulence of the times.

That's how I remember it.

To this...1972, (L to R) Aunt Susan Roth Young, Robin, Dad Jim, James II,
Kim with Little Cousin Scott in front of Robin. We'd made it without a Mom.
Then Bente arrived, November 5, 1972, what a rescue she made for us!

NOW WHAT

Can I do this? How can I do this?

I was trying to make my paralyzed brain get to work. My self-confidence was facing a tremendously difficult challenge. These questions and many others contaminated my usual ability to think clearly. Kim and Robin, my two young daughters were crying; their younger brother, three-year-old Jamie, was staring into space with a confused grimace on his little face. After leading into the subject softly, feeling my way as I spoke, I cut to the chase.

"Your mother and I are separating; a divorce is the only choice," I blurted out. They were mighty tough words to spit out to three young kids who now knew that their Mom wasn't coming back home.

The girls had some sense of what was happening as several neighborhood homes had single-parent arrangements due to separation, or divorce.

I continued. "We are going to go it alone; work together and make the best of it, right?" I pleaded. There was no answer, just more tears.

"I've tried. You've tried. We know that, but over the past year things have not been good and you surely must realize something has to be done. We deserve a better life and more happiness around here. That is impossible with your mother carrying on the way she is."

Difficult as it was, I spit the tough words out to my sweet and innocent kids. Fighting back my own tears, which I knew would do no good — I instead struggled to remain strong and positive. I had to convince them that we were doing the right thing.

"You've got to buck up!" I pleaded, I remembering Dad saying those same words when the going got tough back home. His words fit the situation and I was trying my best to do so. Dad's expression helped me in the past when extra strength and courage were needed. I thanked him again, mentally, for that phrase.

It was apparent to me that I must talk with my parents; they needed to know this major change in our lives. I wanted to hear their voices and craved their assurance and support. I hoped their loving and understanding words might help calm our situation. The phone call was dreadfully

131

Jamie, Robin and Kim, played at the family organ at a time when Jim was thinking, "Now what (do I do)?" He's chosen to go it alone as a single-parent and the thought of the responsibility is overwhelming. There was no other option for him.

sad. I wished so not to have to unload more bad news on them. The ugly realization hit them quickly and hard. It seemed as though they lost their lives, but were still living. The phone wires were heavy with emotion; it was difficult ending the call. We had recently lost my brother Bill to cancer; he left behind his wife and three small sons. The previously wonderful life story of the Roth family was in ashes, all around us. I was feeling guilty, sorry and a sense of failure, as I added my predicament to our family's incredible sense of sorrow and loss.

My children's welfare and my career as a Navy tactical pilot were in jeopardy with all that was happening. I couldn't see how raising my kids and being on call for military duty could be compatible. I was on primary call-up for sea duty to a carrier squadron deploying to the South China Sea, for action in Viet Nam. I was the producer and director of this tragedy and I had to pull a genie out of the hat, somehow, or other. It was difficult for me to think clearly; my thoughts were cluttered and jerky. For someone who usually thought things out clearly, I felt myself at a loss. Taking a deep breath helped, but quickly the air was sucked out of me again and again as new realizations crossed my mind. Without an adult to talk and strategize with, it seemed as if I was shoveling against the tide. I was a young Dad with small children, ages nine, eight and three-years-old, caught in a conundrum of gigantic proportions. Other than the Bible perhaps, there were no books to read, that I knew of, to give me direction.

I kept thinking...*Now what?...Hmmm...Now what?* With three little kids staring at me for answers, I had none. It was 1966, in those times, when marriages failed, fathers didn't get the kids.

That's how I remember it.

Epilogue:

In the days, weeks, months and years that followed, I learned many lessons. I learned that time itself can fix things. (Seven years passed before I remarried and brought a "Mom" back into our family). I learned that I was capable of doing much more than I ever dreamed possible. I learned that I had many friends and family who would help us survive the hardships. Most importantly, I learned that my children were capable of understanding, and pitching-in-to-help, more than I could ever have imagined. Kim, Robin and Jamie joined me in creating a tight-knit and hardworking family team with everyone sharing responsibilities. One time, while speaking with me, a neighborhood mom (military wife) compared how things were done in our home with that of a "military compound." That was not so. Our family of four eventually formed an unbreakable bond. Things worked out well in most every respect. We pressed on with our lives and today look back with pride in what we were able to accomplish. Love was the adhesive that held us together — and it remains so to this day!

Dave Roth in the pool, on another occasion,
before his accident and neck injury renamed him "Titanium Man."

WILL IT WORK

The vast majority said not! Jim and Bente were 40 and 27-years-old, respectively, and had known each other only ten weeks. The wedding was arranged for in six weeks; 300 guests received invitations. Nearly every invited guest came to find out if this was the real deal. Did the wedding couple actually know what they were doing?

News of the marriage, on such short notice, had stunned some and amazed others. Jim, a divorced father, had raised his three children alone, for seven years. Bente was a registered nurse, never married and extremely independent. The best estimate on the marriage's longevity was four months; the worst was four days.

The stage was set for an interesting day; no one was disappointed. A party at the country club followed the 2:00 p.m. church wedding. The mood was light, and the guests were ready to party. The friends of the bride and groom came together like wine and cheese. Before the party ended, near midnight, many had made new friends. The groom in Navy mess dress uniform, his children's participation in the wedding party, the innocence of the bride, in her spectacular white gown, and the cutting of the gigantic cake with a glittering military dress-sword created a captivating scene. A happy atmosphere prevailed as the newlyweds remained long into the night to express their appreciation.

It was November; the children were in school and family adjustments awaited. The honeymoon was short. Jim returned to duty as Navy Representative-in-Charge, Grumman Calverton, flying production acceptance test flights in Intruder, Prowler and Tomcat aircraft. Bente folded and stowed her nurse's cap and assumed a new role as wife, mother and domestic engineer.

The newly reorganized Roth family resided in Shoreham, New York, while an expansion to their new home in Riverhead, evolved to better accommodate family growth. An adjustment period ensued for everyone, including the pets. The two cats and two pet rats bonded quickly. None of the humans found the transition especially easy, but time worked its magic.

New quarters were ready for occupancy, after months of delay, but the new beauty and comfort were worth the wait. Moving to Riverhead from

Bride Bente and Groom Jim, glide up the aisle of the Methodist Church, Riverhead, New York, on November 5, 1972 as they wondered, 'will this work?' They were hopeful!

Bente and Jim toast their 36th Wedding Anniversary with hopes for many more happy days.

Shoreham meant changing schools and making new friends. The kids reluctantly accepted the challenge. Kim at sweet-16, Robin at 15 and Jamie at ten-years of age, had to adjust to having two parents watching their every move instead of just one.

Dealing with many changes in their youthful routines was difficult; they did their best. Bente had a "detective's eye" that enabled her to see through things that had previously slipped by. The "adhesive" that held the new family organization together was the arrival of an addition, 14 months into the marriage. Baby David became the family centerpiece. Bente had her hands full, with teenage daughters, a ten-year-old son, a new infant son and a husband flight-testing aircraft, at Grumman, sometimes seven days a week. It was miraculous how unity and understanding prevailed. Individual comfort zones developed as the family worked to establish new traditions.

There were family vacations, ski trips, camping excursions, functions at school, sporting events and trips to New York City. A drive to Estelline, South Dakota, was a must for Bente, who hailed from Bergen, Norway. She had yet to travel to the Midwest, and being an artist, she had a special desire to see South Dakota's plains, farmland, the Badlands and Black Hills.

A tornado warning, just as they arrived in Estelline, ran a chill up everyone's spine, but luckily it was but a near-miss. Bente enjoyed the South Dakota scenery: the fields of flowering flax, the winding Big Sioux River and panoramic Lake Poinsett, where many chapters of Jim's youth unfolded. She found the natives warm and friendly; it was reminiscent of her homeland. The trip from Long Island was a long drive for a short visit, but it created lasting memories.

Back at home, the girls enjoyed relief from the responsibilities of cooking and house cleaning, but they had regular daily chores assigned. With a stepmother who resembled a high school cheerleader, or homecoming queen, their friends marveled at the novelty. However, it was a "tight ship" at home; Dad's Rules didn't change.

Bente was an extremely capable, talented homemaker who kept things on schedule. Her military training and skills as a Navy nurse were factors not known about by many, including her step-children. Her expectations of honesty, respect and discipline were quickly made known. They were qualities that had kept the single-parent family together, in earlier times of struggle.

Jim and Bente have exceeded best estimates on the longevity of their marriage as glasses of champagne "clink" together on the occasion of each wedding anniversary accomplished; their 36th recently slipped by. Life for the family moved through college experiences, military service, marriages, divorces and grandchildren. The original pets went to their reward and replacements came on board. Through it all, the family managed to maintain close ties. *This whole thing is going to work out okay!* Jim has often thought, but never said.

That's how I remember it.

MILITARY LIFE

Bancroft Hall, United States Naval Academy, Annapolis, Maryland was my home away from home from June 1951 until February 1952. It was where we ate, slept, studied and received services. One of the world's largest dormitories, Bancroft Hall seemed like a city in itself. The cannon out front points at Brother Bill's room, while mine was a fifteen minute walk away. We scarcely saw each other.

NAVAL ACADEMY

"So, Mr. Roth, what brings you to Canoe U?"...his pet name for the United States Naval Academy. Mr. Marcus Aurelius Arnheiter was a First Class Midshipman who had just been designated as my "Firstie," as they were called at Annapolis. He and I were thrown together by the system. As a member of the Class of 1952, Mr. Arnheiter was assigned to guide and direct me through Plebe Year; it was his responsibility to see to it that I was a "good plebe."

"My choice of being here at this very moment, Sir, was heavily influenced by my brother, Bill, a member of USNA Class of 1953, and my father. Dad obtained a principal appointment for me from a friend, The Honorable Harold Lovre, Congressman, 1st District, South Dakota." I then added, "I was an engineering student at South Dakota State College, quite content with running around in my levis and saddle shoes, chasing girls with a six-pack of beer under one arm." That, it seemed, may have been the wrong response.

Mr. Arnheiter's body stiffened as he roared back, "So, we have a wise-ass plebe here, do we not? You listen to me, young man...you had better change your attitude and change it fast, or you will quickly find yourself in real serious trouble." He continued, "Trust me, I know all about trouble. I'm a former cadet from West Point, as well as from The Citadel...before I entered Annapolis. I was thrown out of both those 'brand-X' institutions before I wised-up and set my course for success." He sounded believable, even a bit sincere about wanting to help me do the right thing.

Trying not to show fear in my voice, I continued, "I like most things here...the strict military drill, rugged physical fitness training, teamwork and the rapid-fire pace, but Sir, these academics have me frazzled. You see, Sir, I came from a very small high school, in Estelline, South Dakota, where few, if any, math and science courses were available to us. We studied mostly business, history, English and practical subjects. I achieved entrance to the Naval Academy through intense academic training at Northwestern Prep School, Minneapolis, Minnesota, where my Dad was able to enroll me and willing to spend a bundle of money. At Northwestern Prep, we studied six days a week, both day and night, to

141

*Jim enters Main Gate at United States Naval Academy, Annapolis, Maryland,
with a smile on his face, July 1951. It's "I-Day" (Indoctrination) his life changes forever."*

*prep for the academy entrance exams. A grade of 2.5 was the minimum
acceptable grade, and THAT is just what I was able to achieve. You might
call it a miracle, Sir!"*

"Well, my young man, the miracles are over. From now on you will
find your own hard work and attention to detail are the only things that
will keep you here on these hallowed grounds," Mr. Arnheiter blared at me
with his usual threatening tone of voice. He was proud of his status as First
Class Midshipman, only a few months away from graduation, meaning a
regular commission and career in United States Navy.

*"Tell me more about this Second Class Midshipman brother of yours.
Is he squared away, or is he gross like you, Mr. Roth?"* I felt this inquiry
about my brother was most unfair. It didn't feel right that this conversation
should include the matter of my relationship with my brother. He contin-

ued, "Does this, Bill Roth, do favors for you? How often do you Roth Brothers see each other? Must I report this illegal liaison to your Brother Bill's Company Commander?"

I could feel anger brewing in my gut. Why did he have to get my brother involved? I was lucky to see Bill once per week and that was usually in the church party group we'd joined that marched into Town of Annapolis for religious services on Sunday mornings; a privilege all midshipmen rated. We marched to church in formation and were not permitted to talk in ranks. Mr. Arnheiter knew well the church party regulations and procedure at Annapolis.

After taking a moment to catch my wits and to think over what I could afford to reply, I responded, *"Sir, my brother is very cautious with our relationship here at the Academy, not wanting to jeopardize the record of either of us. He is in 3rd Company, 1st Battalion, 1st Wing of Bancroft Hall. And, as you know, I am in 23rd Company, 6th Battalion, 6th Wing of 'Mother B' which puts us about as far apart as we could be."* That seemed to satisfy Mr. Arnheiter for the moment. I continued, *"My brother and I are not close here; he knows little about my progress, thoughts, grades, or activities; we both feel it is best this way."*

The conversation ended abruptly as we realized the time and that we were about to be late for noon meal formation. Mr. Arnheiter and I took off running to catch the brigade formation on the terrace of Bancroft Hall. I knew we would be meeting again in his room after evening meal; this was standard ritual for plebes. No doubt, our conversation would pick up where we left off. I had all afternoon to think about my responses to questions I expected to hear. My head was spinning with challenges ahead, as I carried out the remainder of my daily routine. I would need to know words and tunes to songs I may be required to sing, facts about Navy ship identification and nomenclature, the menu for upcoming meals, spontaneous jokes to tell, sports scores, current national and world news, AND...'How Many Days' (until...Beat Army.) I could not let myself think about how much I missed the easy life back at South Dakota State College. Oh how I longed for the sound of clattering cowbells at State's ballgames. There...it was "Beat the U" (University of South Dakota)...not **BEAT ARMY!**

After eight months of academic struggle at USNA...and having to deal with the likes of Mr. Arnheiter...I gave up the effort; marched out the Naval Academy Main Gate and retreated back to Estelline. Shortly thereafter, I re-entered SDSC. In record time, I earned a Bachelor of Science Degree, in

Saluting, still with a smile, Jim stands next to the Academy's Victory Bell near Bancroft Hall, as his Plebe Summer grinds on and on. Navy beat Army that December and the bell got its rust knocked off.

Brookings, South Dakota, a Navy officer's commission in Newport, Rhode Island, and Wings of Gold in flight school, in Pensacola, Florida. I was off and flying by age 25; it was 1957.

Strange as it may seem, a lasting friendship evolved with Mr. Arnheiter, and it has lasted for many years. Although we both served 20 years of active duty in United States Navy, Marcus retired one pay-grade junior to his plebe, but we don't discuss it and I don't "pull rank."

That's how I remember it.

RESERVIST IN SERVICE

Damn, it's cold, dark and lonely out here. I sure hope a car comes along pretty soon — even if it doesn't stop to give me a lift, I was thinking as I stood road side on US Highway 77. On a Friday night in February 1953, I was hitchhiking south from Brookings, where I was a student at South Dakota State College, to my naval air reserve unit, at Naval Air Station, Lincoln, Nebraska. I was heading south for a regular drill weekend, a nagging monthly requirement I could not miss. Since I had been unable to arrange for a military flight or a ride with another student at State, who was also a naval reservist in training, I had resorted to "hitching a ride with my thumb." The 225-mile journey was much too long for my trusty Cushman scooter, the only wheels I owned.

I'm cold and hungry, there must be someone heading my way — wonder what's happened to the usual heavy Friday night traffic? I kept muttering to myself to keep warm as I turned my peacoat collar up and pulled my wool watch cap down over my nearly frozen ears. The color of my navy blue uniform was low visibility in the darkness, but being made of wool it was quite warm. I wore my uniform to attract attention, hoping a passerby might be patriotic enough to stop to give a lift. So doing had worked well on many occasions. Motorists sometimes went out of their way to accommodate my travel, even paying for my food if we happened to stop for a meal.

Near midnight, after eight hours on the road, I arrived at the air station after "hitching-up" in ride segments along the way with a couple of truckers, a van and three cars. My last lift thoughtfully dropped me off at the main gate. I trotted the last mile to the barracks after identifying myself to the gate guard. I warmed up nicely in my top bunk and slept like a log until 0600 reveille; it came quickly. *Now that wasn't such a bad trip coming down,* I reassured myself as I was shaving, in case we had a surprise morning inspection. *Gosh knows what will happen on the "hitch" back to Brookings, Sunday evening* — I wondered somberly while swiping a polish rag over my spit-shined shoes to remove the accumulated dust layer. Hitchhiking did have risks; my parents disliked my "thumbing" on long trips. Catching rides back and forth from Estelline to Brookings was okay;

the 22-mile trip was "friendly" and folks stopping to give a lift were usually locals — merchants or farmers, sometimes next door neighbors.

I enlisted in the naval reserve to ensure deferment from the draft, so I could complete college, and then earn my officer's commission. The plan was to obtain an education and then serve my country. Dropping out of US Naval Academy, Annapolis, during the Korean War made my local county draft board extremely interested in where I was and what I was doing. Reserve duty at Lincoln turned out to be interesting, educational and sometimes fun. Two of my reserve shipmates, Jerry Gross, Beatrice, Nebraska, and Del Harding, Lincoln, Nebraska, became close friends. We became like brothers and through them I made additional close friends.

Work in the unit took me new places, from being an assistant plane captain on the flight line, to photographers mate striker in the photo lab, then yeoman in the administrative department of Air Wing Staff #76 Squadron. Navy reserve personnel who only met for drills on weekends were known as "Weekend Warriors," and that's what we were. None of the jobs seemed right for me, but I progressed in rate from airman recruit to airman apprentice to airman while attached to the squadron. The advancements earned increased base pay and helped fund college expense.

As a non-rated enlisted person things were okay, but I longed to earn commissioned officer status. For the time being, to earn extra money, I requested and received flight orders (called flight "skins") which authorized me to hangout at the Base Flight Operations counter where pilots came to file flight plans. I spoke up, showing my flight orders, and asked around for clearance to go fly with anyone in any type of aircraft. I wasn't that fussy, I assumed every pilot was a good pilot. When granted space on a flight, I hustled to the flight line to climb on board, and await take-off.

One such unforgettable flight occurred after boarding a WWII era torpedo bomber called a TMB-3 Avenger. I was eager to fly, also a bit naïve. As the plane commander was signing my authorization chit, at the operations counter, he gave an order.

"Sailor, you will be riding aft in the gunner's station." It sounded like a fine deal, but little did I know.

"No sweat," I replied. While climbing aboard the rugged warplane, I fumbled by way aft to my assigned battle station. I quickly realized and was a bit startled to see how austere things were. I had no communications (radio or intercom); no seat in which to strap in. My parachute and survival pack were there, in case serious trouble "broke out." How I was expected

to bail out from such tight quarters, if it should become necessary, puzzled me. In time, I heard and felt the propeller turning and we began to taxi for take-off. When the big round engine went to full power the noise and vibration clued me to hang-on for takeoff.

Once airborne we were on our way for a night navigation sortie to Oklahoma and return. As the sky darkened, my Avenger slid to the rear of the four-plane formation; we were now "tail-end-Charlie." I noted we had no external running lights — a discrepancy that should have grounded the aircraft until repairs were made. *Inoperative external lights...definitely a safety of flight matter...we launched regardless...I'm trapped here for awhile.* I was feeling a bit anxious. Striving to think positively helped and anxiety was replace by a shot of adrenaline. I felt my courage began to build. About that time a new concern struck. *The other pilots in the formation are going to have difficulty keeping our aircraft insight as it slices through the dark night with NO running lights.* My emotions were racing back and forth, but I could say or do nothing to change matters.

Here's something I KNOW Mom wouldn't like. It was a strange thought at the time. *Oh, I just won't tell!* I tried to relax and settle into the situation I was helpless to change and began to enjoy the flight, trusting the pilots knew what they were doing. I was mesmerized by glowing flames shooting from the engine's exhaust stacks each time the pilot made throttle adjustments, perhaps because he was running with the fuel mixture set too rich. I hoped we had ample fuel supply onboard. I had no way of knowing.

Climbing into the tail-gunners turret for a better view, I pulled a heavy armor-plate panel up under my butt, jamming my legs into a weird and uncomfortable position. *Flight pay was being hard-earned this trip,* I reminded myself. Relief didn't come until after landing at home base and deplaning — four hours after take-off. *A ride in a flying coffin, it was,* I joked to myself, not wanting to disrespect the pilot as he signed off on my flight pay authorization chit. The idea of becoming a naval aviator gained significance — it would get me a better seat, up front and better control of things!

Reserve duty involved travel to new venues. During the summer of 1952, while on break from college, it was to "Accelerated Rate Training Camp" at Olathe Naval Air Station, Kansas. Ten weeks were devoted to training in basic and trick military drill on the dusty grinder, marching the leather off the bottoms of our shoes, while enduring the Kansas heat and humidity. Skills learned and knowledge gained during my time at Annapolis made this sailor a "shoo-in" choice for unit company commander. Leading (100) enlisted reservists (mostly college students) effectively was expected; I had no choice but to set a good example and stay out of trouble.

Formal class instruction in naval history, communications, military etiquette, the Uniform Code of Military Justice, health and hygiene and aircraft maintenance procedure took us off the oppressive grinder and out of the elements, but into hot stuffy rooms without air-conditioning. Trainees earning top grades, in academics and military performance, were granted occasional weekend liberty passes; some headed to nearby Kansas City. Back on base, some of the more daring recruits figured out how to illegally enter the Enlisted Men's Club for some cold pitchers of beer. So doing was fun until caught! College fraternity training made the mischievous reservists fearless, skillful and without regard for naval regulations. Troublemakers received restriction if and when their malfeasance was discovered by authorities. Performance records suffered following such infractions. Privileges were few and to be guarded. Working parties were plentiful for those discovered in violation or who couldn't keep their act together appropriately.

The most exciting occurrence, at Olathe that summer, was the crash of a large Navy patrol bomber in a remote area just outside the air station fence. Our company of college lads turned sailor learned proper security watch procedures on the job. Normal training schedules were halted as we assumed our duties guarding and isolating the restricted area at the crash site. As security watch-standers, we were posted on duty until relieved a day later by base security police. Fate of the bomber's crewmembers was never made known to us. We had a sense the crash site contained body parts along with charred wreckage. It was gruesome watching investigators paw through what remained, but it broke the boredom of long hours of tediously standing the watch. Investigating was a secret process — one we were not cleared to know much about. It was great leaving Olathe and returning to the good life at college as September approached, but thoughts of the crash site and investigation were difficult to push out of our minds.

In late June of 1953, came the first of two six-week Reserve Officer Candidate (ROC) School sessions, Terminal Island Naval Base, Long Beach, California. My first leg of travel to ROC School involved a military flight from Watertown, South Dakota, to NAS Lincoln which turned out to be filled with excitement. The two-seat SNJ Texan trainer in which I was being transported crashed at Sioux City Air Force Base while landing to refuel. The J-Bird received minor propeller and wing tip damage during an unintended ground loop on landing rollout, due to an inexperienced pilot's failure to lock the aircraft's tail wheel for landing. A Navy SNB "Bug-Smasher," passenger/cargo plane, was dispatched from NAS Lincoln to come pick us up. Neither of us was injured in the crack-up, but major inspection and repairs were needed before the SNJ could be flown again.

The following day, in a cute little Nash Rambler convertible, Del Harding and I departed Lincoln, heading for California. Space was tight in the Nash, but the anticipation of an exciting summer of training in California made the trip bearable. However, monotonous travel along US Route 66 began to wear on us. The car's radiator had been damaged in an earlier accident, and Del was fairly confident the partial repair he had paid for would be adequate. As desert temperatures became extreme, the radiator boiled over every time we stopped. Replacement water for coolant was difficult to find so we added soda pop in the radiator and drove on. Two young beauties delayed us at Grand Canyon where we had paused mid-day to await better (cooler) driving conditions in darkness. After engrossing in some fun photo-ops, a nice dinner and a bit of necking by moonlight, we kissed the girls goodbye, as every good sailor must do, before deploying. Precious time had expired before we finally broke away. It was well after midnight. We found ourselves heading for California at break-neck speed, hoping to make check-in time by the deadline. Maintaining proper speed was out of the question as Del jammed down on the gas pedal. After hours of driving well above the speed limit, our luck ran out. We encountered a highway patrol car approaching from the opposite direction. A blinding spotlight beam struck us as it passed. The flash of light signaled a little Nash convertible had just become a "vehicle of interest." We frantically analyzed our troubling situation. Without warning, Del "killed' the headlights and took a hard right swerve off the roadway into the desert landscape — we huddled in the dark car behind a clump of sagebrush. The "Del maneuver" was working so far — the patrolman's car was observed blazing down the highway in search of us, to no avail. I had visions of two career bound sailors being locked in a jail somewhere and classified by the Navy as AWOL; not a good way to begin officer training. In spite of this second delay, we did manage to arrive at the Navy main gate on time. It was not by much and we were exhausted from lack of sleep and perhaps just a bit too much adventure for one night.

*Jim with his Dad Les, have a happy day at South Dakota State College graduation,
which cleared the way for Reserve Officer Candidate School,
Newport, Rhode Island, and a Navy commission by the end of summer 1955.*

I felt certain, several times along the way, the little Nash ragtop was never going to get us there. I cursed my choice of driving rather than flying to California. On my return trip to Estelline, I arranged for travel by commercial-air, leaving Del and the ragtop to struggle back home alone.

ROC-2 training had a unique collection of characters. Hundreds of college males, from all over USA, attended with high hopes of earning a coveted commission in the United States Navy. My bunk mate (he drew the bottom while I took the top) turned out to be Jon Lindbergh. He was off-spring of Charles Lindbergh — the brave pilot made famous by accomplishing the first non-stop solo flight across the Atlantic Ocean in 1927, flying his single-engine airplane, *"The Spirit of St. Louis."* Jon was a quiet and laid back shipmate, but a good friend. We helped each other ready kaki cadet uniforms for personnel inspection every morning, for six weeks.

Del and I had some bodacious liberty runs in the Nash on weekends, the only time we saw each other as we were assigned different cadet companies. Authorities must have known it would be best to keep us separated. Although wearing civilian clothing, while off base on liberty, was unauthorized we enjoyed taking the chance and slipping into our civvies to relax. As luck would have it, we made the acquaintance of two new friends early in the summer. We met the gals on most liberty weekends for some fun-filled times. A roller derby at the Rose Bowl and time spent at Knott's Berry Farm helped divert our minds from drill, classes and the tedium of training.

Summer passed quickly. Before leaving we made a one-day training cruise onboard a Navy combatant. Designated an APA, the WWII era troop ship was monstrous. Sailing weather was blue sky with sun and puffy clouds. It was beautiful! Once we cleared the harbor reaching open sea however, large swells developed sending the vessel rocking and rolling. Most cadets were landlubbers, having developed no sea-legs whatsoever. Sea-sickness gripped most of the cadets following a fine noon meal below deck in the mess hall. The "puking line" — soon after — manned the rail as wobbly-kneed cadets deposited their lunch over their gums, and down into the sea. Contrary to the plan of the day, chucking your lunch became the main event for the afternoon. Although not sick myself, I learned an important lesson in seamanship — when vomiting on topside, face downwind to keep the mess off your uniform. Two days following the cruise, we bade farewell and happily headed back to our respective college dormitories or frat houses. ROC-2 summer was complete; ROC-1 would follow the next year for most.

During my four years served as a naval reservist, I earned my Bachelor of Science Degree at South Dakota State College. Graduating SDSC mid-May 1955, I headed to ROC-1 training, Newport Naval Base, Rhode Island, following the 4th of July. Requirements had changed drastically; I found training more difficult and demanding than ROC-2 summer in California. The first posting of grades showed I was failing. I felt academically lost. With added effort I pulled some excellent grades by early August. While most cadets enjoyed weekend liberty, in Cape Cod and around Newport, I remained on base for extra help and serious studying. By graduation, my class standing was much improved; I was commissioned an Ensign, another goal achieved!

Commissioning ceremonies were unbelievably satisfying. I stared in the mirror at my new collar insignia, two gold bars! *Precious gold, just precious* — my gleaming smile told it all. To the first enlisted person rendering me their hand salute, I handed a silver dollar, according to tradition. In the pay line, the paymaster handed over an incredibly large stack of green bills. It was much more than most other fellow officers received. The longevity I had earned during years of duty with Air Wing Staff #76 squadron, NAS Lincoln, had enriched my base pay handsomely. It was time well spent on those dark, cold and lonely nights, "thumbing" for a lift, going north and south along US Highway 77.

That's how I remember it.

Like Father like Son...James Roth II, enters the U.S. Navy, makes
Second Class Petty Officer, and earns performance award. James is shown
here on his ship, USS Sumter, LST-1181, with his sister, Kim Roth, in 1983.

A CALLING

The phone rang, that's how it started. I had recently retired from the United States Navy; at least I thought I had! While wondering what to do next, at age 44, and nearly grown up, the call came. A local Navy League member rang asking for help. It was August 1976; Navy Junior Reserve Officers Training Corps (NJROTC), at Riverhead High School, was about to begin year-three when Captain Herb Carr, Naval Science Instructor, decided to "throw in the towel." The Vietnam War had ended, but the aftermath was felt nationwide. ROTC enrollment was down at many college and university units; several were closing. Building a viable cadet program, at the high school level, was a challenge of enormous magnitude. Riverhead's fledging cadet program stood to lose its Navy charter with no instructor to take charge. I accepted the job for one year; no way was this to be a lasting thing.

Pressure from my wife, Bente, provided the push that convinced me to accept the job. Pleased with the thought of my short workday, she emphasized the frequent school recess periods plus having summers off. Bente promised to pack my lunch and she did. However, we both drastically underestimated the challenge. NJROTC proved to be a serious test of our marriage. I wrapped up loose ends and reported to the school. It was but days to opening; disaster stared me square in the eye. I had no time to prepare; anticipatory thoughts (fear) rattled my brain with panic! *Where do I start? How am I to begin? What do I do to open this new chapter in my life?* Then, I said — *Get a grip on yourself, Roth!*

Normally, the Navy required weeks of instructor training and certification, before seeking employment as naval science instructor (NSI). Navy, State Board of Education and School District waivers were granted so as to have an instructor in place by the first day of school. The "USS Riverhead" steamed on schedule; cadets made muster and my instructor credentials were approved — some months after the fact.

Naval Science class attendance was down; fifty percent of the students who had signed up to be cadets failed to show up. Some of the partially trained and experienced senior cadets dropped out when they heard Captain Carr had unexpectedly detached. The cadets seemed to want nothing

*The Corps of Cadets of Riverhead High School, New York, Navy Junior ROTC,
show their stuff on Memorial Day during a parade through town.
Jim follows in trail while bursting with pride in the cadets he learned to love.*

to do with the new guy, CDR Roth. Some juniors and seniors remained, but even those few had doubts about their new NSI, who wore but three gold stripes on his sleeve (a Navy Captain wears four.). The newly reporting cadets, mostly freshmen and sophomores, had no idea what the program was about. It was a strange mix; we all seemed to be wrestling for control. *Get a grip; take control,* I told myself. Resisting panic while struggling for more self-control, I reached back for techniques and ideas that had worked well in past experiences. I had no associate instructor even though require-ments called for a minimum staff of two qualified and retired Navy persons. I had no clerical or secretarial assistance available to me as NJROTC class-rooms were located across the street from the high school, in a well-worn portable building behind the junior high school. My assigned "go-to-guy," Dr. Stanley Krause, was District Head of Special Education with offices located two blocks away. The high school principal and district superinten-dent were feuding over the logic of the US Navy-Riverhead School District co-sponsored program's existence. I wondered, night and day, how in the world I was going to get this questionably seaworthy vessel out of dry-dock and underway.

Spotting a telephone booth close at hand, I slipped in, donned my "Su-perman" suit and flew directly at the challenge. No naval officer "worth his oats" would do less. Arriving early, getting home late, some days failing (forgetting) to fit in lunch, I gave the program my best. So as not to appear ungrateful, I'd sneak the unused brown lunch back into the refrigerator when I arrived to be used another day. There was little time to call for help, write for Navy assistance, or to visit the head for personal calls of nature.

The weeks passed swiftly and after each night of correcting papers and lesson planning, I'd fall into bed exhausted. Performing five classroom instructional periods per day; conducting drill instruction, uniform issue and inspections; ordering films, supplies and more uniforms; chasing absentees, calling parents, keeping records and filing, found my Saturdays and Sundays added to my work week, in order for me to stay afloat and on tops of things.

During holidays and recess periods, I took co-ed groups of cadets on extended orientation trips by chartered bus, rented vans or onboard Navy airlift flights. Occasionally, I drove school busses for short distance cadet trips — until transportation policy changed, outlawing me from doing so. On other occasions, cadet trip chaperones shared driving chores in leased vans. Eventually cadets began to realize how dedicated I was to the success of Riverhead's NJROTC program. They were gaining pride and I was gaining respect. Cadets and parents began to express their appreciation for the work I was doing to develop better students, responsible citizens and effective young leaders. I began to sense a bright glow. I made myself believe it was a "light at the end of the tunnel." It was long in coming, but wonderful to see.

Slowly, painfully so, the school's NJROTC enrollment grew, attracting its share of the finest kids in school. Grooming standards improved, pride evolved and the cadets eventually became role models in school and in their community. Onlookers at town parades went from scowling and turning away as the Corps of Cadets passed in review to applauding and cheering as the high-stepping and immaculately groomed cadets came into view. The Town of Riverhead acquired love and respect for the Corps for the thousands of hours of community service cadets provided each year.

The many helping hands represented by the Corps served the poor, sick, churches, service clubs, senior citizens, charities, town and school system. Cadets in uniform assisted with successful functions throughout the year – even when school was not in session. "Cadet Pride" was evident and people enjoyed their presence and work ethic. The community responded by sponsoring cadet activities and by presenting annual awards to cadets with exemplary performance. Rotary, Kiwanis and Lions Clubs came onboard as did Elks and Moose Lodges, most car dealers, some banks as well as other businesses in Riverhead. The American Legion, Veterans of Foreign Wars, and Disabled American Veterans organizations, as well as the Daughters of the American Revolution sprang forward with funding and awards. A number of private individuals also gave cadet scholarships to cover transportation and fees for summer leadership academies and camps. Outside support came from every direction; I was inspired and grateful seeing so much local recognition for the Corps, year after year.

When an associate naval science instructor (ANSI) was located and hired, the cadet program was able to expand and strengthen after school activities to include competitive drill, trick rifle, color guard, fitness and academic teams. Riverhead NJROTC became "the threat" in competitions both regional and national. Riverhead cadet teams competed at United States Naval Academy and Villanova University, in college level competition. Nothing they had previously experienced matched the cadet challenges at this level. Riverhead brought home its share of awards, consistently.

The Corps traveled on training cruises to Naval Mini-Boot Camp Orlando, Florida; Marine Corps Mini-Boot Camp Parris Island, South Carolina; and orientation trips to Washington, District of Columbia; New London, Connecticut; Philadelphia, Pennsylvania; Annapolis, Maryland; Jacksonville, Florida; Pensacola, Florida; Charleston, South Carolina; Cape May, New Jersey; Newport, Rhode Island; Boston, Massachusetts; Norfolk, Virginia; and New York City, New York.

Selected outstanding cadets earned scholarships to summer leadership academies in Norfolk, Newport and Idyllwild, California. Cadets made summer cruises on Navy ships to Europe and ports of call along the Atlantic seaboard. Exceptional cadets were occasionally permitted to take a day off from classes to board Long Island and New London based Coast Guard vessels for orientation training in near by Long Island Sound. Cadets were also permitted to fly indoctrination flights on board New York Air National Guard and US Navy aircraft when available. Helicopters from the National Guard came to school, operating from nearby athletic fields, to give cadets aviation experience and orientation flights.

Incredible opportunities to inspire and educate cadets were available, based on imaginative planning and the ability to schedule. Military flight crew personnel worked excitedly and professionally with the young cadets. Numbers of Riverhead businesses and service organizations continued to give substantial amounts of financial support and awards to the Corps of Cadets in return for cadet willingness to give thousands of hours of community serve annually. Community financial support supplemented funds received from the school district and Navy for the local NJROTC Program. Riverhead was the envy of many other competing units that had little to no similar respect and support from their communities.

NJROTC was hands-on; cadets who bought into the program had the experience of a lifetime. Those who did not perform well often missed much of the excitement. Thirty percent of the Corps of Cadets membership left the program during the school year for various reasons. Unqualified commitment, self-discipline and loyalty were required to be successful and of value to the unit. Dishonesty, cheating, fighting, insubordination, use of tobacco, alcohol or drugs and chronic absenteeism were not tolerated. Cadets were expected to uphold military conduct and military grooming standards both in and out of uniform. Wearing the prescribed Navy uniform of the day properly, throughout the school day, was required every Tuesday. A stringent personnel inspection was conducted during each class period, either on the parade field or in the school passageways during inclement weather. Personal inspection was mandatory as well as an important part of the cadet performance grade.

Senior Naval Science Instructor, Commander Jim Roth, USN (Ret) on an orientation cruise with his NJROTC cadets from the Riverhead High School, New York, finishing room check with a smile. His cadets were among the best in the business and their achievement records told the story.

Cadets could fail the quarter for poor aptitude, regardless of their academic grade.

Leadership was a calling for me; I stayed with the cadets for 20 years. Riverhead earned repeated national honors from the US Navy, achieving "Top Unit" and "Naval Honor School" recognition year after year. Outstanding cadets attended top colleges and universities on Navy, Army and Air Force ROTC scholarships; others attended US Naval Academy, US Coast Guard Academy, and US Air Force Academy. Hundreds of former cadets serve today as adult leaders and good citizens in varied capacities. Many have kept in touch long after graduation from RHS.

I was surprised, but most pleased to accept the very prestigious "Educator of the Year Award for 1995" presented by the Riverhead Community just prior to my retirement. Many outstanding young cadets, whom I'd had the privilege to lead, sure taught me well! I found it difficult saying farewell to the Corps of Cadets as I detached from "USS Riverhead." I departed with a lump in my throat and a tear trickling down my cheek. "A calling" it was.

That's how I remember it.

HITTING BOTTOM

I made an attempt — really I did — but it was a failure. For a long time, it was painful to think or to talk about it. That was over 50 years ago and still, I have an occasional dream of being there to make another attempt. Won't my mind ever let go? I don't think it's going to until I die.

I've often thought...*had I stuck it out a bit longer, I probably would have made it. My older brother, Bill, made the same attempt — it worked for him.* We did many things the same. As kids, we ranked second in our high school graduating classes, we were successful athletes, budding leaders among our peers, and we liked doing many of the same things. We were twins, born two years apart on the same date. Yet, his attempt worked and mine did not.

I entered United States Naval Academy, Annapolis, Maryland, as a plebe, June 1951. Bill was succeeding at Annapolis as he sailed along nicely in his third year, as Second Class Midshipman. Plebe meant "lower than dirt." We were challenged to perform well enough during plebe summer to academically and militarily earn status and title as Fourth Class Midshipman. Things started off pretty well. Physical fitness training, military drill and learning "Navy-speak" were okay – I could do those things and I was doing them quite well. Time spent learning military drill while a freshman Air Force ROTC cadet at South Dakota State College gave me an advantage over rookie plebes with no previous experience in military drill and rifle manual. I had attended at SDSC, Brookings, South Dakota, earlier while awaiting appointment to US Naval Academy.

Plebe summer days were oppressively hot and humid and jam-packed with strenuous activities. Rest stops were few and privileges were nil. We were hustled by US Marine Corps personnel and senior midshipmen from pre-dawn until long after sunset. Butts were dragging and activities were endless during what seemed like "eight days" per week. There was no let up in tempo from June through early September when those of us who survived plebe summer's grind were permitted to join the mighty Brigade of Midshipmen. Thus we continued our rigorous year of academics, physical fitness training and mind games, plus BEAT ARMY, as lowly 4/C Midshipmen!

Navy did BEAT ARMY in football in December and soon after the long awaited Christmas leave period finally arrived. But, I was worn down, discouraged and ready to toss in the towel. Academic grades were not good in spite of my having to drop participation in sports in order to attend mandatory "stupid study" sessions. Midshipman grades were posted openly and weekly on the company bulletin board. The quality of scores and grades being earned by individual midshipmen were no secret. My marginally acceptable academic performance was there for all to see. Lieutenant Commander Clark, our company officer, summoned me for conference. He enthusiastically and pointedly encouraged remaining on the academy grounds over Christmas recess. He practically guaranteed that so doing would salvage my plebe year by my display of loyalty to the cause and my willingness to participate in intense sessions of academy remediation that would be made available. He informed that 150 of the 1,000 plebes who had entered with my class in June had already bailed out and headed back home. Realizing that I wasn't alone in my academic misery, I decided to give up trying. Having totally lost confidence in myself, I soon made the decision that my academy days were finished. I was facing failure like I'd never before experienced. I felt alone and severely depressed for the first time in my life.

Mom and Dad heard my decision while I was home on Christmas leave with big brother, Bill. I broke the news to him during the train ride from Washington, D.C. to Brookings, South Dakota, where we were met by Mom and Dad. Bill was disappointed, perhaps a bit devastated, but he promised to let me break the news when I felt the time was right to do so. I knew breaking the news to my parents was going to be the hardest thing I'd ever done. We looked sharp stepping off the train together, like twins, in our service dress blue midshipman uniforms. There were smiles, hugs and handshakes, but inside I felt terrible.

It was difficult coming out with the right words, but I did it. I announced to Mom and Dad that I was quitting at Annapolis, on my third day home. Being home in my own bed felt nice, but sleep wouldn't come until I'd unloaded the sad news. Our family Christmas season was rather glum that year. I did more than my share of drinking while partying through the holidays. The booze didn't help one bit. I felt rotten inside about my decision and how it had to have disappointed my parents. They were good about it, showing more understanding than I had anticipated.

Our parents returned us to Brookings to catch the train back east as the holidays ended. A long and tiresome train ride, while anticipating what was to come, was unpleasant for two midshipmen brothers soon to be split apart.

My having to leave Bill behind, and the realization that we would most likely never serve in the US Navy together, were the most difficult aspects of my impending self-induced departure from Annapolis.

Back at school, I ignored the books and wasted study time. My mid-term exam grades were as horrible as I had intended. By early February, my failing academic status created considerable negative attention. The mid-year academic board convened to evaluate midshipmen with unsatisfactory performance. The waiting area, outside the conference room, had few empty seats as midshipmen sat humbly staring at one another awaiting their name to be called.

"Midshipman Fourth Class, James Roth, please enter," a firm voice announced. Weak-kneed, I rose and stepped off smartly, knowing my fate would soon be known. I stood at attention feeling somewhat overwhelmed and very much on display before the longest conference table I'd ever seen. Its plush armchairs were filled with senior officers wearing uniforms with gold-braided sleeves running from their cuffs to their elbows. All eyes were focused on me, I felt as low as one can get, yet I was standing straight and tall.

"How could I have let this happen to Jim Roth? Perhaps I should never have made the attempt," were thoughts that raced around in my head. I was treated respectfully as questions were asked and answers were given. The board chairman asked if I would consider becoming a "turn-back," meaning I would return to the academy in June to enroll and begin again as a member of the incoming plebes. I paused, before making my respectful reply.

"No Sir, I don't feel that would be the best thing for me. I would just like to leave now. Thank you for your consideration."

That was the end of it, I saved a few other thoughts I could have expressed. I tried to keep it simple. It took some time to process me, those were long days of waiting. Within two weeks, I was once again a civilian. I left the academy grounds through the same majestic main gate where I had entered nine months earlier. My baggage in hand with a set of paid travel orders, I headed out on the long lonely trek to Estelline. While heading home, with my tail between my legs, something I was told as a child

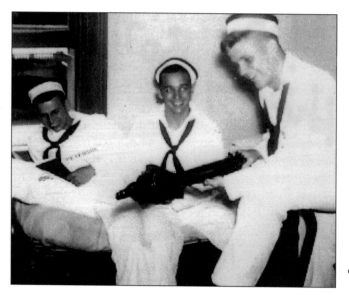

It was a rare 'light moment' during Plebe Summer at United States Naval Academy, Annapolis, Maryland, 1951. Plebes (L to R) Dick Peterson, Glenslaw, Pennsylvania; Jim Roth, Estelline, South Dakota; and Jim Nation, Birmingham, Alabama, are caught in a candid shot, smiling while they clean their drill rifles in quarters, at Bancroft Hall.

popped into my head – *"If at first you don't succeed...try, try, again!"* But first I needed to recharge my batteries. Back home in Estelline was the best place for me to make that happen.

After pouting and licking my wounds for a couple of months, I decided to re-enroll at South Dakota State College. It was 1952 and the Korean War was blazing. I had no doubt the Hamlin County draft board, upon receiving notification of my departure from the US Naval Academy, would elevate my draft status to Classification 1-A. Jim Roth would be quickly moved to the top of the selective service list. I would become prime for military draft orders.

A fellow student at SDSC invited me to join his reserve unit at Naval Air Station Lincoln, Nebraska, offering free transportation to Lincoln for monthly drill meetings. I accepted the offer to further ensure my military draft deferment until I could complete my studies for a college degree. By August 1955, a Bachelor's Degree, an officer's commission and orders to Navy pilot training were in hand. Things looked better for me and I was happy.

In summary, I don't regret my attempt at USNA. "I now think I could have made it" – words from the mouth of a late bloomer.

That's how I remember it.

POTPOURRI

MAIDEN VOYAGES

A boat is often referred to as "a hole in the water into which you pour gobs of your money," and that reference is not far from a brutal "truth-ism." Our boat came along as replacement for my love of flying. When Bente announced that even though she was my loving wife, she would never set foot in an airplane, with me at the controls, but would go fishing with me anytime in a boat we called "ours," a boat search commenced. While shopping together, we quickly settled on a stubby, but wide Cobalt runabout powered by 185-horsepower Merc-Cruiser 10 (inboard/outboard). The vessel was a marine beauty manufactured in the State of Kansas, USA. Naming her was a no-brainer; she is our *Maiden USA.*

Maiden is perfect for Peconic Bay, but can be a bit of a challenge on Long Island Sound, especially when strong winds take command. Her knife-edged deep-V hull rides smoothly, as it cuts through the bounding waves. It's always best to keep a keen eye on weather, especially wind velocity. With few exceptions, time spent onboard has been enjoyable. She slips easily into and away from the dock and trolls at just the right speed for fishing.

When fewer than ten-days-old, while on a demo run with family onboard, *Maiden* had her first and only casualty. As we sped into Flanders Bay for a look-see, with 12-year-old son, Dave, at the helm (with me onwatch), we struck a small island obscured by an extremely high tide. Passing over the scarcely submerged island cause a thud, a jolt and a roar, startling all five of the souls on board. Fortunately the quick stop to examine things revealed minor damage so we slow-cruised back to the marina, arriving safely. The scary incident proved the accuracy of the salesman's pitch. *Maiden* had just proven to us that she was more durably constructed than most other boats on the water because of the unique molding process used in producing the hull at Cobalt Boats, Kansas. We could have had a catastrophic marine accident, with loss of the craft, or much worse. Thankfully, we had only a bad scare and a bit of inconvenience. One week later, after repairs to her out-drive assembly and the propeller, our shiny new boat was back in service, while USA took care of the claim.

Seems it's a slow day of fishing from Maiden, in the Peconic River, Riverhead, New York. Dave and Kim Roth keep their lines in the water, ready for some action.

Skiing is great with the *Maiden* towing; she has both power and speed to spare. Two skiers can easily enjoy darting through the waves riding side by side. Water-skiing and the power *Maiden* packs are a very happy marriage.

Fishing is *Maiden's* specialty, as her slow speed is just right for luring the catch to the hook. Her gunwale is high and "landing the catch" is always an exciting experience. Pole-holders provide an option for the slow times, but fighting fish on the hook is a thrill many shipmates have enjoyed from her cockpit.

Up on the step at 40-miles-per-hour, brings *Maiden* back to shore in a hurry. Fuel economy, not being her best attribute, does mandate judicious use of the throttle. With her openness, a fresh breeze and blazing summer sun, exposure is assured.

Maiden sleeps through the winter in a shrink-wrapped cocoon, but look out for her come summer; she's a "lovely" while rocking and rolling in wind and waves. Few things top a day onboard, with the thrills and spills of skiing or the race of your heart with an oversized fish raging its struggle to remain "out of the boat."

I've noted lately the newer models have "slicker" lines, prettier bells and louder whistles, but with 23 seasons under her belt — *Maiden* continues to delight us, while flaunting her original power and class. The hundreds of hours of running time and the countless fish that have flopped on deck don't seem to have aged her much. In spite of increasing shop labor rates and fuel prices at the dock — *Maiden* keeps us right on pouring! Can't wait to launch and get underway.

That's how I remember it.

NEAR CAREER

"Gentlemen, start your engines!" The starter, with a raised voice, bellowed the announcement over the public address system.

I was thinking, *Oh boy, how I wish I could.*

The crowd in the packed grandstand screamed and cheered as the beautiful open-wheeled race cars roared their engines and began to roll. With their open cockpits you could see the expression on the driver's faces.

It was a career that only came near, but not near enough. While sitting with Dad, as a seven-year-old youngster at the Minnesota State Fair, I'd chosen the all black #8 car as my favorite to win the heat race. The racers roared around the track raising clouds of dirt that drifted softly onto the crowd. I was thrilled to be at my first-ever auto race. On the checkered flag lap, while entering the third turn, the #8 car locked wheels with a bright yellow racer in an attempt to pass for the lead. In a flash, as if in slow motion, the shiny black car left the track — flipping high into the air, end over end. It disappeared from view, over the high-banked turn. Silence struck the grandstand filled with spectators. The race announcer stopped talking. Eventually, fans began to speak in hushed tones as a voice on the public address system tried to comfort everyone's worst fears. We had all witnessed the driver falling from the cockpit of his sprint car as it tumbled through the air, out of control. The crash ended racing for the day and fans slowly left their seats hoping for more word on the driver's condition. No information was forthcoming. Sadly, we learned from the newspaper the next day, death was the #8 racecar driver's fate.

The dreadful sight of that speedy, shiny black racecar flying through the air remains indelible in my mind to this day. Though I felt sadness and disappointment, an aggressive speed-seed was planted in my heart. I have been an auto-racing fan since.

Years later, a small group of businessmen in Estelline, South Dakota, my hometown, built a dirt race track, not long after World War II ended years of austerity. As a teenager, I could get to the track quickly, in our small one-square-mile town. I was a "racer" on my bike, whenever I heard cars turning laps. There were no gates or fences to hold us back at the track. Kids gained access quickly and easily. It became a new place to hangout.

*Dynamite Dan Turbush, many times Champion at Riverhead Raceway, New York,
spins some pace car parade laps. Jim, in the right seat, holds the Colors
for the Nation Anthem. It wasn't competing, but it was a thrill and
most likely as close as he will get to a car racing career.*

I left for college before getting a chance to strap on a helmet and grab
the wheel of a racer. College years presented challenges beyond those of
oval speed and were more critically important to my chosen career path as
a Navy pilot. Otherwise, I would have been hanging out in the pits at the
new track bargaining for a shot at being behind the wheel — it wouldn't
have mattered in which car.

The speed-seed matured in a different way when I became a naval aviator, after college. I spent a 20-year career going fast, but not on a race
track. Speed made my adrenaline pump as I raced about the sky, occasionally to speeds reaching Mach 2 (twice the speed of sound). Back on
earth I purchased go-carts. My four children were taught driving skills as
we informally raced together. Go-carting quickly became a fanatical family
sport. Sad was the day I chose to part with those two swift little "beauties."
I have wished many times I hadn't sold out. Some years later we gained a
fifth child who has yet to learn to drive. We could still be enjoying those
go-carts.

My annually renewed NASCAR license allows me to hangout in the pits at a Long Island raceway on Saturday nights, in summer. I also hold season tickets for major NASCAR races at Richmond International Raceway, Virginia. The speed-seed hasn't wilted one bit over the years.

Once while returning to New York from a visit to the races at Richmond, I made a quick stop on Route 301 for a kind gentleman who was flashing blue lights at me from atop his patrol car. My prompt reaction to his signal to "pull-over" cut me no slack. Following a brief, but meaningful lecture the well-groomed highway patrolman handed me a State of Maryland summons — "Speeding – 90 MPH in a 55 MPH zone!" I was shocked to see such numbers in print! The ride was going along so smoothly. It seemed so non-threatening.

After collecting my thoughts, I motored on more cautiously realizing the highway is best a place for rational thinking rather than "oval speed." The officer made his point quite effectively. I had, however, enjoyed my short, but reckless burst of speed with sunroof open and breeze blowing me about. The wide open and straight stretch of Maryland's Route 301 was too inviting. I felt the irresistible urge to "air-out" my BMW!

To this day, I'd "give my fortune in a minute," if I could become a race-car driver. But...my dear wife says NOT!

That's how I remember it.

Mascara loves the Christmas tree. He is the best at re-decorating, by playfully knocking ornaments to and fro. He is "Boss Cat.

PET LOVE

It all started so innocently with a casual comment from my wife.

"Why don't we buy your Mom a miniature poodle puppy for her birthday?"

We were in Estelline, South Dakota, visiting my parents, while on leave from Navy duty on Long Island, to celebrate Mom's 63rd birthday. Our family was noted for being a bunch of pet lovers, but recently Mom had been diagnosed with allergies associated with animal dander, from pets that shed their fur. She had been advised by her doctor, to avoid pet animals that shed. With knowledge of the problem, from her medical background, my wife, Bente, suggested the "poodle puppy solution." Poodles are okay for people like Mom, because they don't shed their fur. Instead, poodles must be groomed and clipped regularly to maintain the beauty of their coats.

It was the eleventh hour—the day of Mom's birthday. We quickly, and secretly, perused the daily newspaper in search of sale ads for "Miniature Poodle Puppies." The two of us then slipped away, motoring off on a hunt for Mom's surprise gift, a "champion" black miniature poodle pup. It would be a big surprise as Dad wasn't at all in favor of the idea; we knew that. There was a birthday dinner planned at 6:00 p.m., a command performance of sorts. We knew we must be in our place at the table by that time. Heading north for Watertown, 30 miles distant, looked like our best bet. After having no luck we telephoned ahead, then drove to Sioux Falls, 110 miles south, where we struck gold on the first stop, at a private home. After completing paperwork and the purchase, we make a quick visit to a pet supply store for puppy needs. Then it was a hard and fast drive north to be back in Estelline, on time. The 225-mile "poodle puppy mission" was a solid success, even though we did pull into the driveway a few minutes late. We were excited and pleased with the sweet puppy we had been able to find.

Before anyone could utter a complaint about our tardiness, out popped "Fondue" from her spanking new carrier box—the little black girl dog took care of things from that point. Puppy love struck everyone, especially Mom. Dad was a bit chagrined, but cracked a slight smile as he saw how happy

Bogey loved the gold chain with ID tag hung on her neck
for special occasions. It caused her to prance and act with best manners.

Mousse III and Truffle II, mini-poodles from the
same litter, rule the roost around the house; we share a lot of their love.

Mom was with her surprise birthday gift. He was not certain the idea was a good one as he had said previously - No longer having a pet simplifies our lives! In time, Fondue and her puppy-ways melted his heart. There was no problem!

Back on Long Island, after our visit with my parents, it became evident that we needed our own black miniature poodle. My dear wife, Bente, had been married into our ready-made family for less than a year. I had been a single-parent with two teenage daughters and a ten-year-old son when we met. But we had no dog. The idea of getting a puppy evolved from the difficulty we had leaving Mom's cuddly birthday surprise behind.

It wasn't as if we had no pets. "Frick" and "Frack" were part of our family; two lovable and entertaining pet rats. "George" was our trusty Siamese guard-cat, and "Licorice," black with white vest, was Bente's dear-cat. When we joined in marriage, we merged our pets, but there was no dog. In short order we found "Mousse," a cute black male miniature poodle puppy. It was 1973, thus began our family tradition of owning miniature poodles that exists to this day. The names of the ten who followed in Mousse's puppy tracks include: Mousse II, Truffle, Gucci, Trifle, Tiffany, Touche, Bijou, Bogey, Truffle II and Mousse III, which includes the cute batch of puppies delivered secretly by Truffle in our master bedroom closet. There were sad deaths, from accident and sickness, along the puppy trail, but there were also happy new arrivals. Our house has had at least one miniature poodle on board for the past 36 six years.

Both of the pet rats succumbed near the end of our first year of marriage. Domesticated rats are known for a short life-span. First, Frick died from a virus apparently caught from one of the kids. Not long after, Frack became listless with similar symptoms. He soon followed the trail to "rat heaven."

On the day of the first rat casualty, Bente, telephoned to report the bad news while I was at work with the US Navy staff at Grumman Aerospace Corporation, Calverton, New York. I was airborne, piloting an F-14 Tomcat on a production acceptance test flight at the time. From my office, a fellow naval officer, Lieutenant Commander Don Sharer, took her call. He promised Bente I would be notified of the death notice without delay. Don strived to sound a sympathetic tone as he sensed she was somewhat upset.

While clipping along at near the speed of sound, high in a layer of cirrus clouds, near 35,000 feet, a radio message came that momentarily returned my mind to earthly things. It was LCDR Sharer sounding very official with seriousness in his speak.

"Hey Boss, I have a message from Bente...over?"

I wondered for a second, or two, as this was most unusual. She so rarely called me at work. I anxiously awaited his reply.

"Go ahead, Don."

"The rat died."

"Roger that."

I acknowledged, knowing I would have some explaining to do, regarding Bente's message, once I was back on deck. Few knew we harbored pet rats.

I thought for a few seconds what Bente must be feeling. She no doubt was hoping I wouldn't blame her for not doing enough to save our dear sick, Frick. I wrote a quick note on my test card, Remember to thank Don, and explain (when back on deck). My mind quickly snapped back to testing the Tomcat, he was my pet at the moment.

When I returned home that evening, I found Bente feeling very sad. She had learned to love Frick and Frack while adjusting into our married life with all of its "attachments." When free from their cage, the two followed her around, sat in her lap and on her shoulders, sometimes hiding behind her long hair. Sadly, the sudden deaths put an end to having pet rats. After a family vote was taken, no replacements were found.

A year or so later, "George" took ill and died. Unfortunately, "Licorice" caught the same bug and died as well. "George" took the blame for killing "Licorice" who was forced to join our clan when Bente came to live. "Lick" eventually adjusted to our family, but remained a bit leery around the children. Both cats avoided the rats and seemed a bit resentful of their presence. Sweet and friendly poodles took over our hearts and minds so the mourning period for the deceased cats and rats was relatively brief.

As luck would have it, more cats and poodles have joined our clan and, as of now, we have two of each—dogs and cats. Our pets get along quite well together, sharing food and water dishes almost harmoniously. All of the pets receive much love and attention. It's returned in kind. I can't imagine home life without pets and not having to oversee their shenanigans and attempts to rule. Where has time gone? We have now enjoyed 36-years of pet love and marriage together. Life is good and it goes on and on.

That's how I remember it.

ABOUT THE AUTHOR

Jim was born James Frank Roth, in Sioux Falls, South Dakota, on 22 September 1932. He moved to Estelline, South Dakota, with his family in 1934 where he grew up, attending kindergarten through twelfth grade. After taking a stab at being a midshipman at the United States Naval Academy, Annapolis, Maryland, in 1951-1952, Jim dropped out to enroll at South Dakota State College, Brookings, where he earned a Bachelor of Science Degree as a journalist, in May 1955. He served with the naval reserve at Naval Air Station Lincoln, Nebraska, while in college and earned a commission, at Reserve Officers Candidate School, Naval Base Newport, Rhode Island, in August 1955. As an Ensign, he entered basic pilot training in Pensacola, Florida, and advanced training in Corpus Christi, Texas, qualifying as a pilot in tactical jet aircraft. He pinned on Navy Wings of Gold, in April 1957.

During his 20-year flying career Jim served duty in numerous capacities. He was a carrier-based nuclear weapons delivery pilot, a basic training

Jim Roth, writer and author.

flight instructor in SNJ Texan aircraft at Pensacola, a tactical squadron flight instructor in A6 Intruder aircraft at Oceana Naval Air Station, Virginia, and a production aircraft acceptance test pilot in A6 Intruder, EA6B Prowler and F14 Tomcat aircraft, both at Naval Air Rework Facility, Naval Air Station Norfolk, Virginia, and for the Naval-Plant-Representative-Office, Grumman, Bethpage, Long Island, New York. Jim served as the Navy-Representative-in-Charge and Director of Aircraft Acceptance, at the Grumman (Calverton) Airfield production/testing complex, January 1969 to September 1975. He spent interesting and challenging years during the evolution of numerous major aircraft programs including the A6E all-weather attack bomber, the EA6B electronics countermeasures (jamming) aircraft and the F14 supersonic fighter. All were aircraft carrier-based tactical weapons system assets important to the defense posture of the United States. Jim's flying and active duty career ended in retirement September 1975 with rank of Commander. He'd logged 5,600 hours of pilot time and 330 carrier arrested landing without a serious mishap.

Jim began a second career in naval education as Senior Naval Science Instructor at Riverhead High School, New York, Naval Junior Reserve Officers Training Corps (NJROTC) unit, September 1976. His second retirement followed an exciting and rewarding 20-year career working with Navy cadets at RHS, in June 1996. Jim was recognized in 1995 as the Riverhead Community's *Educator of the Year*. He remembers that instructing and leading junior ROTC cadets was different than flying, but just as challenging.

Jim lives with Bente, his wife of 36 years, in Setauket, Long Island, New York. They are guardians of 16-year-old, April Cumley, whom they have raised from infancy. April, a child in need, came into their home for her safety and well-being. She has stayed and is now a permanent part of the family. Four grown children, Kim, Robin, James II and David, have married and have families; the grandkid-count is now at five.

That's How I Remember It, is a continuation of Jim's, *Memories of Estelline*, published June 2006. His sense of humor, writing voice and attention to detail remain the same. Be certain to read both books of Jim's memoirs; he will be glad that you did, and so will you.